THE BAGHDAD COOKBOOK

A contractors' mystical culinary survival guide

With recipes & stories from some of the toughest soldiers and security professionals from the far corners of the world.

Alan Boyd

with
Robbie Stevenson & Scott Greig

The Baghdad Cookbook

PEGASUS PAPERBACK

© Copyright 2023
Robbie Stevenson

The right of Robbie Stevenson to be identified as author of
this work has been asserted by him in accordance with the
Copyright, Designs and Patents Act 1988

All Rights Reserved

No reproduction, copy or transmission of this publication
may be made without written permission.
No paragraph of this publication may be reproduced,
copied or transmitted save with the written permission of the
publisher, or in accordance with the provisions
of the Copyright Act 1956 (as amended).

Any person who does any unauthorised act in relation to
this publication may be liable to criminal
prosecution and civil claims for damage.

A CIP catalogue record for this title is
available from the British Library

ISBN-978 1 91090 377 3

Pegasus is an imprint of
Pegasus Elliot MacKenzie Publishers Ltd.
www.pegasuspublishers.com

First Published in 2023

Pegasus
Sheraton House Castle Park
Cambridge CB3 0AX England

Printed & Bound in Great Britain

About the author

Alan 'Al' Boyd was born in Belfast, Northern Ireland in 1962 where he remained until he was seventeen years old. In 1979, he joined the Royal Marines serving with them until 2003. In 1982, Alan deployed with 45 Commando RM during the Falkland Islands War and saw further deployments to: Hong Kong during the period of handover in 1997, Granada, Norway, Northern Ireland and the Caribbean. He specialised as both a Ships Marine, Coxswain and Clearance Diver on multiple Royal Navy vessels.

In 2004, Alan moved into the private security sector working in the Middle East as a Team Leader for multiple international companies and clients. In 2008, Alan received special thanks from the US Army for assisting in a military road traffic accident, after a main battle tank had overturned during operations. Alan's security team were the closest supporting asset to the accident, who secured the tank and assisted with the wounded until recovery arrived.

After working in the Middle East, Alan returned home to his family and his beloved Scotland. In 2012, he was diagnosed with leukaemia and spent the next twelve months in chemotherapy at the Nine Wells Hospital in Dundee, before passing away at home on July 12th, 2013.

This is Alan's first and only book…

About Robbie & Scotty:

Robbie Stevenson was born in Portsmouth in 1969 and moved extensively around the globe before he turned fifteen years old. In 1986, he joined the Royal Marines serving with 45 Commando RM, 3 Commando Brigade and as an attached rank to the Special Boat Squadron. He saw operational service in Iraq during the 1991 emergency, 'Operation Safe Haven' providing a security screen for the persecuted Iraqi Kurds in the north, with further deployments to Norway, Northern Ireland and the Middle East.

After leaving the Royal Marines in 2000, Robbie worked for an event management security company in the UK before moving into private security sector and deploying back to Iraq/Syria with a number of international security and humanitarian aid organisations. In 2020, after sixteen years of working in the Middle East, Robbie retired from private security and resettled in the South West of the UK.

Scotty Greig was born in his beloved Glasgow in 1970 where he remains to this day. After leaving school, he joined the Junior Leaders Infantry Battalion before his sixteenth birthday. After completing a year's training, he joined The Royal Highland Fusiliers as a Private at Redford Barracks in Edinburgh, as part of the Royal Guard at Balmoral.

For the next nine years, Scotty served in multiple operational theatres that saw him deploy to Northern Ireland, Kenya, Germany, Canada, Belize and as part of the allied forces during the first Gulf War 'Operation Desert Storm,' in 1991. In 1997, Scotty left the army.

Scotty then spent the next few years driving heavy goods vehicles across the UK and Europe, before moving into the private security sector in Iraq with international security companies. After they saw his value, company management moved Scotty quickly up through the ranks from Team Leader to Project Management, looking after multiple million-dollar security projects, managing personnel and equipment, all under high-risk conditions.

Contents

About the Author	5
About Robbie & Scotty	7
Foreword by Alan Boyd, written in Baghdad, Iraq, 2009	11
Foreword by Robbie & Scottie, written in 2019	17
Acknowledgements	21
Recipes & Stories	24
Measurements	25
Jack Daniels Alabama Pie	27
No Runners-Up	31
Baghdad Stovies	42
Scotty's Best Friend	44
Memories From Iraq 01	55
Simple Flat Bread Pizza	57
Bandit Country	60
The Basrah Omelette	68
A Moment on the Lips	71
Convoy All Day Breakfast Roll	81
The Gift that Keeps on Coming	84
Memories from Iraq 02	95
The Contractors Curry	97
Memories of an Accidental Tourist	100
Nepalese Bean Stew	109
Dead Men Tell No Tales	112
Chilli Jackets	122
A New Sheriff in Town	125
Memories of Iraq 03	132
Gurkha Chicken Cutlets	134
The Gentle Assassin	137

Convoy Crew Beef Stew	146
It's a Mine, It's a Yours	149
Hobo Meals	156
The New Beginning	158
Memories of Iraq 04	172
Fried Bread 'A-La Convoy'	174
The Dirty Dogs of Al-Fatah	175
Pan-Fried Mushrooms at Dawn	189
Contact	191
Melted Malted Bars	202
The Private Volunteers	204
Baghdad Munch Brunch	215
The Real Expendables	217

Foreword by Alan Boyd, written in Baghdad, Iraq 2009.

I've been in Iraq, working with a British private security company since 2004. We do everything from protecting high-profile diplomats, moving them in and around Baghdad, through to escorting military equipment from one end of the country to the other. The convoy escorting work was at one time, without doubt the most dangerous job in the world. We are a mixed bunch, coming from all corners of the globe and all with different backgrounds, different heritage, different stories. The private security industry recruits worldwide, unlike army regiments who tend to often recruit locally, and Iraq is our common denominator.

We work out of a location codenamed 'Victor-2,' which is a series of secure 1960s-style villas, a central location in the heart of Baghdad (if you will). However, please don't get carried away with the 'villas' idea, it's more like Fawlty Towers meets the Middle East just after the Blitz. The electricity turns off some ten times a day; the water is contaminated with cholera; we have rats the size of cats, and the six inches of green stuff in the bottom of the disused swimming pool contains bacteria still waiting to be named.

It wasn't long before I realised that the most popular and most respected members of any security team weren't those with the toughest war stories, but strangely enough, it was those guys who could create something nice for dinner.

Over the years, I have worked with some truly exceptional people and learnt a great many new skills, which has come in handy as we have all been shot at and blown up so many times, I've lost count. I have made some wonderful friends here and a brotherhood that lasts beyond time and space. Sadly, we have also lost many close comrades along the way, who will never see another sunrise, or taste another pint of beer.

Much has been written about Iraq, mostly by some ex-super soldiers telling how everyone around him was struggling, except him and although it was all going wrong (and they had been dropped completely in the wrong location), none of it was his fault. Or, some shiny ass officer who was sitting miles behind the action. There are no inflated egos here; this is from the boots on the ground, warts and all.

Away from home we have been forced to learn a different set of skills and, this book is a true story of learning to survive, as real as March or Die. This is a book of soldiers and contractors working abroad in arduous conditions with a guide to how we learnt to cook or starve. A series of stories where fancy kitchens, professional chefs and kitchen equipment was not a luxury we had.

In this, we have put together a collection of our favourite recipes, not just from Baghdad or other corners of Iraq, but from conflict zones around the world; all of which are well tried and tested. But, if you are looking to calorie count or to lose weight, then I am afraid you've come to the wrong book. The recipes and design are the ability of using whatever was available and to hand at that time, especially when much of it was scarce or non-existent.

At the time this book was written, things were a little different then to how they are now, time has moved on, but back then we didn't have the luxury of a set of scales or measuring equipment, so all measurements were approximate using everyday items such as: a cup (an actual cup), tablespoon, teaspoon, a slack handful or a finger pinch. You get the meaning... In turn, we will introduce you to each member of the team, or former military friends, who will explain his recipe step by step. Then, in the time it takes the dish to cook, he will tell you a true story of his time as a soldier or security professional and give you his personal safety or practical awareness tips.

Disclaimer*:*

All the stories (at the heart of it) are factual and as they were seen on the day. And, although this is not a diary or historical document, some of the names have been changed to protect the guilty. Where people are still actively involved in live operations, names and details have been omitted. There are no pictures of people with brown paper bags on their heads, or black masking tape over their eyes that's just silly! Oh! and we do take the piss a lot, so don't be offended.

We hope you enjoy the recipes, meeting our friends and hearing their stories as much as we have, I know I am privileged to have graced their company. They are all men you won't meet every day...

Dedication

This book is dedicated to my good friend, Gordon McPherson from Oban, Scotland. Gordon was just nineteen years old when he was killed on the 12th of June 1982 during the assault by 45 Commando Royal Marines on the mountains of Two Sisters during the Falkland Islands war.

Gordon, my friend, I have climbed every mountain, lived and loved well, because you never got the chance to. In my heart, I have tried to live my life for us both. I am sure many of us who survived that night feel the same. The first toast is always to absent friends... "So, here's to absent friends, Gordon."

Alan Boyd
Sept 1962 — July 2013

It is not the critic who counts; not the man who points out how the strong man stumbles, or where the doer of deeds could have done them better. The credit belongs to the man who is actually in the arena, whose face is marred by dust and sweat and blood; who strives valiantly; who errs, who comes short again and again, because there is no effort without error and shortcoming; but who does actually strive to do the deeds; who knows great enthusiasms, the great devotions; who spends himself in a worthy cause; who at the best knows in the end the triumph of high achievement, and who at the worst, if he fails, at least fails while daring greatly, so that his place shall never be with those cold and timid souls who neither know victory nor defeat.

Theodore Roosevelt

Foreword by Robbie & Scotty written in 2019

Many years earlier—before the selfish bastard went and died on us, Alan had been sitting in a roasting hot Baghdad team house, perched on the edge of his bunk in his straining undercrackers. At the time, one of his testicles was shyly peeking outside of his boxer shorts, as if looking to see if the coast was clear before completely rolling out of his stifling sweaty shorts. Just then, the immortal words parted from Al's lips and we two held our breath, *"I've got an idea, lads…"* at which, the two of us glanced at each other, raised our eyebrows and thought exactly the same thing at the same time, *"… here it comes."* Alan then continued and pitched to us, his latest and most creative idea to date for *The Baghdad Cookbook*. At the end of his forty-minute salesman-like pitch, and after slurping our way through several cups of putrid, over-brewed local tea, he asked us both what we thought of the idea.

As with most of our previous thought schemes around the campfire, involving dreams of mass fame and fortune (of which there had been many), we thought this was just another one of our hare-brained ideas that would, in all honesty, eventually fizzle out and be pushed to the recesses at the back of our minds before being forgotten. But… a few days later after he had pieced together the first chapter of his book idea, we realised he was serious. And not long after, when he had sent us the first rough outline draft copy of the book, we knew then he was double serious.

Unfortunately, Al never got the chance to see his dream through. Only a short time later he returned to the UK and was diagnosed with Acute Myeloid Leukaemia and was taken to hospital. Alan then spent the next twelve months battling round after round of chemotherapy inside the amazing Ward 34 of Dundee's Nine Wells Hospital. It was a heart-wrenching period but, during that time there were moments of brilliance where we thought this Captain Hurricane figure had beaten his illness only to see it sadly return weeks later. Not once did we ever hear him complain, nor did he ever stop smiling that infectious smile of his. Instead, he only sought the positive in everything, remaining ever optimistic to his situation and take the weight of everyone's sadness on his own already burdened shoulders. To this day we have never known such bravery. Sadly, it wasn't to be and after a year-long monumental battle, he succumbed to the leukaemia and passed away peacefully on the 12th July 2013 at his Arbroath home surrounded by his family and friends.

(*Robbie*): The name Boyd was not all unfamiliar to me. I had heard his name bounding around the Royal

Marines even before I left the service and plunged into that huge pool that is Civvy Street. However, it had taken a cold and wet December evening in 2004, down in the southern Iraqi city of Basra for our first *actual* meeting. I had just taken my first sip from a can of smuggled-in English ale, when the door to our makeshift team bar burst open, almost coming off its hinges. Suddenly, in walked a knuckle dragging man-type-thing, with close-cropped hair and shoulders that you could have launched Harrier Jump-Jets from. Right there in the dingy smoke-filled room, a million miles from home, our hands clasped in handshake and I knew in my heart of hearts we were destined to become close friends.

(*Scotty*): Some four years later, having been moved up to Baghdad on a project, I met the short-on-legs Irishman, who at the time could be seen standing scowling at inanimate objects and anyone brave enough to catch his glaring eye. He had with him the lanky streak of barn door that was Robbie and we instantly went from a double act into a trio of friends, becoming a tight-knit little unit.

With favourable winds and the gods smiling down upon us, over the course of the following years, the three of us worked project after project after project, job after job after job. Often, we worked ourselves through inhospitable hell-on-earth locations and all manner of things nasty set to maim or kill us, yet all the while coming through some of the toughest days you ever want to have in this lifetime, or the next.

As our time as a trio, trickles down in Iraq and draws to a close, it seems only fitting to finally fulfil our best friend's dream of completing this book for him. Not only as a testament to Alan and recounting some incredible tales about him, but sharing with you, the reader, some of the people we have met along the way and including their own personal stories too. Much of what you read is in Alan's own words taken from his original first draft or has been added in his spirit as it was described to us at the time. We have left it with only minimal changes to the original vision, and of course, as with any good tale, there is a little artistic license taken here and there… ahem! but as Al always said, *"Never let the truth get in the way of a good story."* We hope you like it.

RS & SG — 2019

Acknowledgements

This book is the vision of one, the completion by two, and is a testament to the many with the culmination of an everlasting friendship that has held firm over both time and distance. In writing this book, none of it would have been possible without the great love and support of many people—too many, in fact, to fit onto one page so we have kept it short.

Firstly, we would like to thank Alan for being the most amazing and most incredible human being we have ever met. Your kind heart, compassion, your warmth, your generosity had no limits. It is with you in mind that we live, love and continue our days in the hope of being half the man you were. We are all certainly more blessed for having you in our lives, shipmate. You are a true gentleman and are dearly loved and terribly missed.

We would like to give a deep appreciation to Senga and the Boyd family for allowing us to pick up the baton and complete Alan's dream from where he left off. Right from the start, you welcomed us into the family and it is with great love and affection that we say a huge thank you.

To all of the doctors, nurses, medical professionals and the hospital supporting staff, who tirelessly work at the Nine Wells Hospital in Dundee on the Leukaemia Ward, with special mention to those who attended and treated Alan while he was receiving chemotherapy. Your passion and dedication for what you do, for all patients who come to Nine Wells Hospital seeking help, is an inspiration to us all and it is with this in mind that this book is dedicated. A huge debt of thanks goes to: Pam Neil, Lea Dobson, Lee Newman, Trisha Connor, Elsie Angus, Cheryl Martin, Shirley McCall, Paula Parker.

To all of our own long-suffering wives, children and families, we give endless love and thanks in your support of us rascals, who had some inexplicable calling to run off to the Middle East and play silly buggers. For all your patience, your understanding, and for standing by us when we came home at the end of long rotations, bringing all our emotional baggage with us. By rights we should now be on a basket-weaving course, drawing on the walls with crayons between our toes and dribbling down our fronts; words will never be enough for putting up with us. Thank you.

To those who have helped and supported this project, a huge thank you to: Gilly, Suren, Andy, Hitman, Daz, Tom, Tony, Steve, Ben, Gaz, Dave Moody, Desi Vanstone; The Royal Marines Association, RSM Ollive & CSM Asson (45 Cdo RM), Steve Millan and the Royal Marines South Atlantic

Association; Rhiannon for proof reading our work, Marina for her keen eye.

To ArmorGroup, who took a chance on three scallywags such as we and threw us together inside the great melting pot of Iraq. To: Ian, Phil, Kev, Chips, Tim, Baz, Clint, Steve, Stu, Stevie, all of whom for recognising our potential and allowing us to remain together. To all the friends we made along the way, of which you are many, and to the 79 who never came home.

To security contractors across the world who protect, defend, guard, escort and stand watch, we give a big shout-out.

…And finally, to the men and women of the British Armed Forces, you are the best in the world. The military gave us a sense of belonging in a challenging world; you gave us a family, a purpose, a sense of duty and direction; you aimed high and you got us there. You showed us what it was like to belong to something truly amazing, unique and exclusive. People who have never served, nor heard the battle call can truly understand the bond that the military weaves between us, it is only a slim few that will ever know its tight-knit embrace. To all of you, regardless of the colour of your hat, the unit patch on your shoulder or your regimental history, we are bonded by a common cause (PAM-45) and so to you, we also salute you.

To each and all, we give thanks…

Recipes & Stories

Measurements

Living in Iraq in the immediate aftermath of war presented its own unique challenges, especially when it came to cooking. Without the luxury of scales or fancy equipment, many of the teams had to improvise and learn quickly, often through mistakes, just how much to add or mix in. Below is an approximate scale of how we measured ingredients for the recipes in this book.

Dollop: Used mostly for oil-butters-savoury liquids and has no known exact measurement. This generally tends to be known as whatever fits the job at hand. It can be approximately as small as a spoon-sized portion or as big as a biscuit-sized portion. In many cases, it fits the individual's need/choice. Similar names could be: splurge, plop or splash.

Pinch: Using finger and thumb to take hold of the ingredients

Bunch: Using an open hand, grab the ingredients in a loose pinch-like grip. Open grip allowing access to fall away.

Cup: Use a tea cup, preferably a china tea service type cup.

Mug: This generally tends to be a standard size coffee mug

Tablespoon (TBLS): standard size dessert spoon

Teaspoon (TSP): used generally when making tea/coffee.

Jack Daniels Alabama Apple Pie

A rare and special treat after an arduous mission out on the ground and where time is an even rarer luxury.

Prior to prepping: Half fill a whisky glass with sultanas and cover them with Jack Daniels. Steep overnight.

BASIC PIE PASTRY:
5x tablespoons cold water
2x cups all-purpose flour
½ teaspoon salt
2x tablespoons sugar
⅓ cup unsalted butter

MAIN PIE FILLING:

⅔ cup Jack Daniels Tennessee Whiskey
5x medium-sized cooking apples
½ cup unsalted butter
½ cup whiskey-soaked sultanas
1x cup sugar
3x tablespoons cinnamon (if available)

PIE TOPPING:

⅓ cup sugar
3x tablespoons dark-brown sugar
¼ teaspoon salt
⅓ cup all-purpose flour
⅔ cup unsalted butter
½ cup pecan halves (if available)
½ teaspoon cinnamon (if available)

"I know someone is going to ask where you find Jack Daniels in Iraq… Just find an American oil worker and you have found your Jack Daniels…"

PIE PASTRY:

In a mixing bowl, add the flour, salt, and sugar. Cut the butter into ½ — inch sized cubes. Then add the butter to the flour mixture and, using your hands, mix the ingredients together until it looks crumbly. Now add approximately 5x tablespoons cold water, one at a time, and continue mixing after each addition. After the fifth tablespoon has been added and mixed, the dough should merge into a lump-sized ball. Bring all the dough together into a disc-size shape, cover in clingfilm wrap and place in a fridge for at least 1 hour.

After 1 hour, remove the dough from the fridge and lightly flour a surface. Using a rolling pin, or equivalent work the dough into a circular shape approximately 5mm thick, and large enough to cover the bottom of a deep-dish pan. Transfer dough to the pan and lay in the bottom, crimping the edges with your fingers and using a fork to prick the bottom of the dough.

Preheat your oven to 180-200 degrees.

PIE TOPPING:

In a separate bowl, mix together the sugar, salt, flour and cinnamon (if available) for about one minute until completely mixed together. Chop the butter into small pieces, add to mixture and blend together with fingers until mixture is crumbly. Once completed, then mix in the pecans (if available). Now cover and refrigerate until ready to use.

Main pie filling:

Separately peel, core and cut the apples into 2-3mm thick slices and put to one side. Melt some butter in a large pan over medium/low heat. Once the butter begins to bubble, add the apple slices and sauté for approximately 5-6 minutes before removing them from the heat. Add and stir in the cinnamon, sugar and whiskey-soaked sultanas over the apple slices and return to the heat, simmering the apples over low heat for a further 1-2 minutes. Now remove the apples carefully from the pan using a perforated spoon and place the slices apart from each other on a baking sheet or plate, avoiding heaping the apples together. Leave the butter-sugar mixture in the pan and add in the Jack Daniels whiskey into sugar mixture. Simmer mixture over medium heat until alcohol burns off for approximately 5 minutes. Then return apples back into the pan and stir to coat evenly.

Now add the apples and whiskey-sugar mixture into the pie-pan crust and avoid over-filling, leave a few centimetres gap from the top free. Add your pie topping evenly across the dish top and place the pie in the oven. Bake for approximately 55 minutes until filling is bubbling and topping is golden brown. Once cooked, remove the pie from the oven and place to one side leaving it to stand for a few minutes before serving. To accompany the pie (and if available) add fresh cream or ice-cream when serving.

No Runners-Up

ALAN

- *Formerly*: Sergeant Royal Marines — Personal Protection Officer — Maritime Security Operator.
- *Saw active service in*: The Falkland Islands war, Northern Ireland, Granada.
- *Seven years' private security in*: Iraq, USA, Kurdistan and Cyprus.

9 Troop, 45 Commando Royal Marines on the move after the battle of Two Sisters, Falkland Islands war 1982. © S. Millan

We landed in Ajax Bay on the morning of 22nd May 1982. We were supposed to have landed under the cover of darkness but two of the big landing craft had bumped into each other in the dark, just off the back of HMS *Fearless* and the ramp on our landing craft was jammed closed. It was a beautiful fresh morning, but very cold as we climbed over the side of the landing craft, into the sea and waded ashore.

Our immediate task was to secure the beachhead at Ajax Bay until the bulk of our stores and equipment could be landed safely, then we were to move off and recapture our primary objective, Port Stanley, clearing any enemy resistance or defended positions, along the way.

The Falkland Islands are pretty devoid of any natural cover and at times it felt like there was practically one tree for the whole island and this was only seen sometime later over by the Governor's house inside Port Stanley. We were ordered to '*dig-in*' with shell-scrapes. We pulled out our entrenching tools and were looking getting stuck in, when one of our troop, a lad known as 'Muscles Bette,' took the first swing with his pick. *Dink!* his pick lazily bounced off the frozen ground hardly leaving so much as a scratch. It was still winter and the ground was a mass of solid ice and frost. Elsewhere, a team of assault engineers then had a go with a fist-sized chunk of plastic explosive (PE) but only managed to blow a hole about the size of a football. This was never going to be a trench war.

As men all along our position struggled to dent the frozen ground, with all of us thinking what to do next, suddenly in the distance, against a light-blue sky, I could make out two small silver dots.

"What do you think they are?" I asked Scutty who was next to me.

"They look like planes," he replied

"Do you think they are ours?" I asked.

"Yeah! They're coming this way they must be ours," he said.

As the two aircraft raced towards us, we could make out the V-shaped sweptback delta wings of French built III-EA Mirages. The Mirages then opened fire with their 20mm automatic cannons sending plumes of water high into the air, before hearing a dink! dink! dink! as the rounds bit through the first ships who were harboured in the bay. This was then followed by; splash splash-splash, dink! dink! dink! as the next ship was strafed with ferocious gunfire. From our positions on the shore, approximately a hundred yards up the beach, it never occurred to me that we were directly in the firing line of the aircraft attack runs and I was mesmerised by the show, like a rabbit caught in a car's headlights.

"Get down you plank!" Scutty shouted as he knocked me hard to the deck.

Scutty was our Section Corporal and one of the old hands in the troop, someone who had seen many years of service and more commonly known as '*an old sweat.*' He had previously volunteered for back-to-back tours of Northern Ireland throughout the late seventies and as a

Royal Marine, he really had his shit in a sock, he knew his stuff. Scutty quickly forgave my lack of naivety and spared me the bollocking I thought was coming, but my lesson was well learnt. When it goes loud, get low.

The two Mirage aircraft then banked hard left, slipping behind some small hills and headed back out to sea...

Thank God they've gone, I thought, but it had only been a practice run because moments later the two silver arrows appeared once more and were lining up for the main event.

"Here they come again," I said to no one in particular and this time they were dropping 500lb bombs as well as firing their 20mm automatic cannons.

The ships in the bay were easy pickings, as they were land locked on three sides and in perfect illuminated daylight. Everything we needed to fight this war was still on board those ships; every round of ammunition, medical supplies and tomorrow's dinner, all of which was still yet to be offloaded before then being ferried inland and taken ashore.

I was one of the youngest and least experienced Marines on the beach that morning but even I knew things had gotten off to a bad start. Just then from the other side of the bay, two Royal Navy Sea Harriers dropped in on the action. Forget the local county air show or Maverick and his Top Gun, those were not even close to what was unfurling. All safety was off and there were going to be no runners-up in the middle of this event. As we watched from the shoreline, the Mirage aircraft were flying low but the Harriers were almost skimming the tops of the waves as they chased after the Argentinian Air Force fighters. In a desperate attempt to escape, the two Mirages broke left and right but it was already too late. Unbelievably at a height of less than fifty feet, the Harriers flipped upside down and as they rolled back over again, a volley of rockets from under their stubby wings sent the Mirages crashing hard into the sea.

The two Harriers still wing tip to wing tip, pulled up slightly and banked hard left as they flew a single lap of honour around the bay before heading back out to sea and back to their ship. I'm sure the pilots heard our cheers of appreciation even over the roar of their two huge Rolls Royce engines and suddenly we all knew we were still in the fight.

The following morning, we began the long yomp to Port Stanley. My Bergen was top heavy with everything a young Marine needed to fight a war: ammunition, food and something warm to wear. All the extra rubbish you carried throughout training or on exercise, that all got buried at Ajax Bay. It didn't rain every day; luckily for us, some days it was too cold to rain and it only snowed. We yomped across peat bogs, stone runs, and bastard grass, so called because the grass arranges itself in close densely packed thick tufts, the size and shape of World War Two German helmets. You can't put your foot down flat on it and when your equipment weighs almost as much as you do it's hard to stay on your feet. Every time someone stumbled or fell over, all you would hear was "bastard!"

Step by step, day by day, we drew ever closer to our objective, Port Stanley. By now only two enemy positions stood between the Port and us. Mount Harriet to our west and Two Sisters about twelve miles directly to our front, both of which were heavily defended.

On the night of the 13 June, under cover of darkness, 45 Commando moved into position for the attack on Two Sisters. Off to our right we could see our sister unit, 42 Commando, had already begun the attack on Mt Harriet. Attached to us were an Artillery Fire Control Team, a Captain and a Sergeant. We paused, crouching low and in the darkness, as they directed 105 mm artillery shells from 7 Battery Royal Artillery onto the enemy positions.

Having looked down, there on the ground by my feet was a piece of string, I picked it up and began winding it around my hand like the good Marine I was, until I saw that the other end of the string was hanging from the Fire Control Officer's pack. As I approached him, he was holding his radio mike in one hand and hitting it with the other.

"I've lost bloody comms with the gun line," he growled to his Sergeant. I then tapped him on the shoulder and handed him the neatly coiled length of string.

"This was hanging out your Bergan Sir," I said quite proudly as if doing him a massive favour. There was a look of abject horror on his face as he looked down at my hand. The piece of string was in fact a twelve-foot-long trailing wire antenna from his radio. The Sergeant stepped between us quickly taking the wire from my hand and threw it hard back out along the ground and I silently slipped back into the anonymous comfort of darkness.

Back in my position, the shadowy camouflage silhouette in front of me, slowly stood up and began moving off so I followed along. Sometime later we stopped again; this time, we peeled off from the rear and moved towards the front and as we did, I knew this was to be the start line for the attack that was coming, because we were now forming a line in reverse order. I was suddenly gripped by a hand from the darkness which held me by the shoulder for a second. It was my Troop Sergeant.

"You were here on the recce last night young'un, weren't you? Do you think you know your way to the right-hand edge of the start line?" he asked me. I looked down and recognised some of the landscape and the holes I'd fallen down, and some rocks I'd tripped over the previous evening.

"Yes," I whispered and pointed off to my right along the dark berm line and into the darkness.

"Well off you go then," he whispered.

This was it, whatever came next, this was what we had come all this way for. As quietly as possible, we slid off our heavy packs and then arranged our kit for a fight. Fresh magazines on the left side of your belt, hand grenades on the right. The last bits of biscuits or bits of saved ration pack chocolate all got quickly scoffed, as we didn't know when the next meal would come.

We lay flat and still against the cold, hard ground anticipating what was to come next. I never saw or heard them, but low and fast through the blackness of the night sky two Harriers were screaming towards us. The harriers dropped two 500lb phosphorous bombs directly onto the enemy position; this was just so the artillery could see what they were shooting at. The flashes from the explosions looked like two huge bolts of lightning erupting from the ground and for the first time we got a good look at what we were up against. The ground to our front rose steeply; it was peppered with rocks and large boulders with a series of enormous plates, the type similar to the scales on the back of a huge prehistoric animal. If you could have designed a naturally defendable position, then this was what you would have drawn. It had everything: a steep slippery slope scattered with boulders, interlocking arcs of fire and good natural cover. Suddenly it was the turn of our 81mm mortar troop. Our mortars had a ridiculously high trajectory as if they fell from heaven and there is no place to hide. Off into the distance I could hear the sharp jagged splinters of shrapnel ricocheting between the rocks close by pinging away.

Steadily moving forward, we made our way up the hill and then almost on cue the enemy opened fire. I could hear at least three .50 Browning heavy machine guns barking out their heavy chunky rounds as the sky lit up with streaks of red and green tracer; with nearly all of it coming in our direction, the noise was utterly deafening.

At this point we were now beginning to take casualties and our advance halted. I lay on the ground flat and still noting some incredibly brave Marines running forward through the deluge of incoming fire recovering the wounded. The Marine beside me winced in pain. I knew him well; we had previously been in recruit training together just two years earlier. He had a large piece of what looked like scrunched-up tinfoil sticking through his upper arm and pinning it deep into his chest. Gordon, another young Marine near us, was dead. Gordon was crouched in a fire position with the butt of his rifle still in his shoulder looking over his sights, but there was no movement and his life was gone.

We were seven and a half thousand miles from home on the side of a mountain in the rain and darkness, outnumbered and pinned down in a murderous crossfire. *It never looked like this in the movies*, I thought to myself. Then suddenly, directly overhead, I heard the 'whoosh!' of artillery shells. The first couple of rounds landed short and to the right of us, but were quickly corrected which then saw 7 Commando Battery right on target. The big 105 artillery rounds were smashing hard into the base of the enemy position; I could see bodies, equipment and chunks of rock being thrown high into the air.

Our training had taught us what was coming next and we needed to be almost on top of the forward enemy position when the artillery stopped, or we were just going to be pinned down again and in a world of hurt. With 9 Troop, Zulu Company on the far right-hand side of the attack, we pushed quickly uphill and along a large V-shaped stone run that provided some cover from the heavy concentrated enemy fire but was in danger of separating us from the rest of the attack. As fast as we could, weighed down with belts of ammunition, we made our way onto a flatter piece of ground about 30 yards to the right of the enemy position that was still hidden in total darkness.

We were now at right angles to the attack. We watched 8 Troop thrust up over the hill with bayonets fixed and throwing hand grenades like they were serving tennis balls at Wimbledon. The General-Purpose Machine Gun beside me opened up with long bursts, as did the rest of the troop right into the flank of the enemy positions. As 8 Troop drew closer, we switched fire as they leapt across the first of the enemy shell scrapes dropping grenades and firing into the trenches as they moved.

The attack continued in what seemed a timeless age until we spotted Argentineans in the rear dropping their kit and running. Nobody fired on them and we let them go. And suddenly it was all over as the firing died down to nothing and we held the Mountain. In the aftermath we painfully lost nine Royal Marines that night in just a few hours of fighting, a heavy loss for such a tight-knit unit.

For the rest of us, as the sun came up, it marked the start of a new day, yet there was still work to be done. The injured were brought together to be cared for; the Argentines separated from our own. The dead were very gently laid out, correctly identified then carefully covered. Winn Jones, the Padre said some nice words and soon it was time for us to prepare to move on again.

We lined up the Argentinean prisoners and all of their walking wounded along a natural rock wall feature to protect them from the harsh wind, rain and their own friendly fire. They were shattered, utterly defeated in every way and looking forward to going home. No matter the advantage in numbers it's difficult for any conscript army that doesn't want to be in a fight or try to defeat a professional well-trained army that is cherishing every minute of the fight. At nineteen I learnt a great lesson in self-defence: total attack.

Al's Personal security tip: *"Violence is seldom the answer but when it is, it's the only answer."*

Baghdad Stovies

Winter nights in the open desert can be extremely cold. This recipe was quick, easy, filling and very tasty. A classic comfort food dish when time was short and the next mission was just hours away. Simple, easy to prepare and popular among the convoy escort teams when time was limited. For the best results of this classic delicious dish, you need a Scotsman to help create it. I know in Scotland they make Stovies with good quality minced beef and using beef dripping traditionally, but unfortunately there aren't too many herds of Aberdeen Angus wandering around in the Iraq desert…This was always a hit for big cold hungry lads.

INGREDIENTS:

1x tin of corned beef
1x onion chopped roughly
Enough potatoes, peeled and slice approx. 1 x medium to large per person)
2x vegetable or olive oil
1x beef stock cube
1x beef Oxo cube
300ml water
Salt & pepper to season

METHOD:

Warm up a medium-sized pan on the cooker adding a small dollop of oil and add in your chopped onions. Cook the onions thorough until they turn opaque/translucent. Don't be afraid to slightly overcook the onions, which will add more to the flavour. Add in the beef stock, sliced potatoes and Oxo cube, finally add 300ml of water and bring the lot to the boil.

Stir occasionally and allow the ingredients to simmer. Cook thoroughly until the potatoes have softened and have absorbed most of the stock. Drain the potatoes and add in the tin of corned beef to the mix and mash the ingredients together until it becomes thick and stodgy. Add seasoning to taste and serve hot… Enjoy.

Scotty's Best Friend

SCOTTY

- *Former*: JNCO Royal Highland Fusiliers & Recce Troop Sniper, Personal Protection Officer and highly skilled PSD Driver.
- *Active service*: Belize with the DEA, Northern Ireland, Kuwait 'Operation Desert Storm'.
- *Security:* Worked for sixteen years as a private security professional in Iraq
- *Additional*: Likes to think he is a direct descendant of Rob Roy MacGregor.

One of the many jobs we have as a Private Security Detail (PSD) is moving officials, diplomats and VIPs around the central Baghdad region of Iraq. Baghdad, or

'Baggers' as we more commonly call it, is a giant melting pot of people, districts and diversity all squeezed in to about a 204 square kilometre radius and all with a dense population of just over seven million people.

As in most armed conflicts, the battle lines are seldom straightforward or simple. The political climate and religious divides between Sunni, Shi'a and Christian runs deep with a great many frightened people all looking for stability and leadership. Unfortunately more often than not, that very leadership remains commonly corrupt.

Along the way our job of staying safe is seldom easy and the situation can often become extremely volatile with little or almost no warning at all which many of us consider as a tinderbox atmosphere for anyone working in the city. An experienced personal security team can read the signs and look for combat indicators instantly and then raise or lower their stance to match the threat without ever dropping their guard. Over aggression is often more dangerous than not reacting at all, with the general idea being to remain as low in profile and as inconspicuous as the situation allows. But, the second it goes loud and noisy, everyone must be prepared to take any action necessary to extract both your client and your team away from that danger.

No true professional soldier or security professional will ever deliberately endanger themselves or intentionally harm anyone who isn't a threat, but when the life of your client, your team and you are on the line, it is imperative that you must be prepared to do absolutely whatever it takes to protect life. If anyone ever had any kind of problem with that then they were in the wrong job. This wasn't a tickling contest and we were not plumbers or electricians; if you carry a gun you have to be prepared to pull the trigger.

The Karrada Peninsula in central Baghdad is a predominantly mixed Shi'a and Christian area. In 2009, by Baghdad standards, it was generally considered a little safer than its surrounding areas… but only just. Sited with a modern Baghdad University packed with students and a regional upmarket, prosperous feel about the district, the peninsula is joined to the rest of Baghdad via a series of bridges that span the River Tigris. Central to all this is the infamous 14th of July Bridge that leads directly into the even more infamous Green Zone. This was an area that had been walled off and where most of the international embassies are located, as well as the Iraqi central government.

Many people have a misconception that the Green Zone covers about a third of Iraq, this is purely because most of the world's mainstream news teams and reporters were based in the zone during the 2005-2010 period and was considered at that time a heavily guarded and a relatively safe area.

It was commonly viewed among security teams that reporters merely stood on the hotel roof wearing a helmet and body armour reporting, "*Here we are in the*

Green Zone close to the town of Baquba where all the fighting is taking place..." (actually Baquba is about sixty miles to the north, but with some clever camera angles you can't quite see the Pizza Hut, Burger King and international coffee shops in the street below). After the news piece to the camera was finished, off came the helmet and body armour and it was back to the deckchair with a large vodka and ice, you get the picture.

In all fairness to the reporters, they would hardly be able to show the true carnage and cruelty of say, a mass car-bomb attack where people are walking around on fire and no two pieces of skin on their body joined together, nor would they show a pile of murdered bodies stacked one on top of each other as high as a man is tall with blood running into the gutters. Most of our TV news is broadcast around teatime and no rightful TV station is going to show anything that could put us off our sausage, egg and chips in case ratings dropped off.

As for our clients, they come in all shapes, sizes, and attitudes. Some PSD teams dislike female clients, as it's just another set of problems they can do without; Hanna, however, like a small few, was the exception. In her previous life back in the USA she had been a personal assistant to some high-flying Senator but, here in Baghdad, she was helping to train and organise Iraq's first freely elected democratic government. She was as sharp as a tack, highly educated, extremely motivated and determined to do the best job possible for the Iraqi people. She was tall and slim, possibly in her mid-fifties, in which the years had only slightly dimmed what would have been in her day a stunningly beautiful woman. I could only imagine that she would have left a trail of broken hearts on her travels through the corridors of power back at home.

Hanna was every bit the model client all of us dreamed of having. She was punctual, always turning up on time; she always did what was asked of her without question and just let you (the team) get on with your job without hindrance or obstruction, unlike many other clients who had seen *Rambo* twice and thought they knew more about your job than you did.

It was early one morning that we picked Hanna up from her hotel halfway along the main thoroughfare of Karrada known as 'Route Oilers' which ran pretty much east-west, smack-bang through the heart of the peninsula. I had been tasked as her designated personal protection officer, or 'PPO' as its more commonly known.

Upon seeing her that morning I shook my head. "Hanna… what's with the high heels?" I asked.

She insisted that the shoes were the only thing that would go with her trouser suit and that nothing else she had would possibly match what she was wearing. I then asked if she had a pair of training shoes she could wear.

"Trainers… *trainers*!" she cried, "with this suit, you have got to be joking!"

I quickly explained that in extremis, should a situation dictate, she may have to run a fair distance between vehicles, or escape out of the area.

"You wear the trainers in the vehicle, and we will give you your shoes back when we get to where we are going, how's that?" I asked, before reluctantly but understandingly, Hanna agreed.

I was in the second vehicle and Alan, as the Team Leader of the four-vehicle security move, was up front. We set off without incident and as we eventually approached the 14th of July Bridge with its series of entry checkpoints and we slowed to a crawl as we had practised countless times. Around this time, Iraq Security Forces (ISF) were known to be a little twitchy. As the US transitioned more and more power back to Iraq, the ISF, enjoying a new sense of control, liked nothing better than to flex their muscles and bugger about international security teams for no other reason than because they could.

As we approached the bridge, coming ever closer to the Green Zone, we closed in towards the main Iraqi police checkpoint just prior to the bridge itself. The expectancy of being waved through without issue was our biggest hope, but when the police spotted Hanna through the security vehicle window, our hopes were dashed and we were pulled over to the side and stopped.

Having spotted a pretty foreign female in the car, it became obvious very quickly that the Iraq police decided right there and then that they wanted to search one of our vehicles and of course it was Hanna's vehicle they wanted to search, which was for no other reason than to get a good letch over her. There was no facade of professionalism; they all emerged from their guard hut and just lined up making it clear that they wanted a good look at the girl in the car.

I asked the security vehicle behind us to come up close on our left side and in a trained procedure known as 'cross-decking', I opened both doors between the two vehicles and moved Hanna into the other vehicle before locking the doors. Although this had been the right professional thing to do, it was not what the police wanted to happen and their anger now showed. So now both of the two primary vehicles were subsequently pulled over by the police.

Having moved the second vehicle forward into the search area, everyone alighted from the vehicles and then opened all the doors and stood back to watch the debacle unfold. The little crowd of police officers that had gathered, having now viewed Hanna, slowly started to drift away, possibly bored.

There was about another twenty minutes of pointlessly waiting before a police officer finally came over to start the actual search. There was nothing to find of course; all our weapons and kit were attached to our body armour. This was just an opportunity to mess us around and keep us standing in the sun as payback for denying them their sad little bit of excitement for the day.

At this point, as the police officer deliberately dragged out an excruciatingly painfully slow search of the vehicles, a K9 search dog arrived with his handler, which I thought was just getting silly by now. The dog's handler was a big dark South African chap from another private security company and he turned and asked why we had been stopped, at which point I just shrugged and sighed. At his feet was the ever-faithful search dog that was a wonderful looking beast of a German Shepherd and a big old boy at that.

After more wasted minutes, finally the bored policeman decided he couldn't drag his search out any longer and signalled through the vehicles open back hatch-door with a 'thumbs-up' that it was now the dog's turn.

The dog handler slipped the leash and without any hesitation, the dog, seizing his chance, bounded off at speed. In seconds, the dog covered the twenty feet between where we stood and the back of the security vehicle in around three bounds, actually clearing the last six feet fully airborne. With his final bound, his front paws hit the tailgate and then cleared both the back and front seats with the full might of his force. Whatever the dog had going through his mind at that moment, it had determined that this was now *his* moment and he was going to fully embrace it.

The dog hit the policeman on the back of the head with his mouth open as wide as a striking crocodile as teeth and gums sank in without mercy. The policeman, totally unprepared, broke into blind panic and was then thrown around inside the car like a ragdoll. Arms and legs flew all over the place, and screams came from the car that sounded like something from a Michael Jackson concert. To our utter amazement as the scene unfolded, a pair of trembling hands came out through the vehicles front right foot-well grabbing for the door handle, but instead of pulling himself out of the car, he only managed to pull the door closed on himself. I looked at the rest of the team who were by now in tears, rolling down their faces amidst howls of laughter.

Finally, after what seemed like an age, the dog's handler started a slow, uncaring and bored walk towards the car as if oblivious to the commotion and screams from inside the vehicle.

"Leave it!" was all he said and the dog suddenly stopped his vicious attack, and, with a tongue hanging out of the side of his mouth and a wagging, happy tail, padded back to his handler and stood by his side.

I dropped to a knee and wrapped my arms around the dog's neck and patted his head.

"Who's a goood boy then… yesss you are, you're a goood boy aren't you!" I then reached into my side pocket and pulled out a handful of protein bars and started feeding them to the dog. "Oh yes, you're a clever boy!" I added to the dog, who wagged his tail even more happily at the prospect of treats.

Hearing the commotion, but slow to react (as usual) the rest of the police now arrived back on the scene.

Some went over to help the policeman, who was still in the vehicle moaning loudly, but one police officer went to grab me by the arm in an attempt to pull me away from the dog, possibly because I was making such a fuss over the animal. In one swift reactionary motion, I pulled down hard and fast slipping my arm away and turned towards him, squaring myself right up to the police officer. In the background I heard my team also turn to face the officer as one unit and began positioning themselves ever closer to me. There was no threat, no moment of anger, no words, but the situation was not lost on the officer who thought better of trying to be the big man. Instead, he waved us away trying to restore some semblance of order to the shambles that had just occurred.

The moment was quickly over and as we got back to the security vehicles and loaded everyone in, there was blood, dog drool and shreds of blue uniform all over the seats which I thought was going to take forever to clean the mess up.

We went past The 14th of July Bridge checkpoint three or four times a week and I always made sure my large furry friend always had a good supply of cold fresh bottled water and a few spare protein bars... Strangely that was the last time we were ever stopped at that checkpoint...

Scotty's personal security tip… *"Always sit at the back of an aircraft as an aircraft never reverses into mountains."*

MEMORIES FROM IRAQ 01:

Whose bright idea was this then? Scotty pretending to be in the huff! We had just moved out of a nice four-star hotel in central Baghdad with three cooked meals a day, your own room with air conditioning, TV, internet, a fridge, double bed, balcony and a laundry service... for this and a camp in the desert only partially constructed, beds made of packing crates and food so lousy the locals wouldn't touch it... and we loved it! © A. Boyd

MEMORIES FROM IRAQ 01:

Typical individual's PSD kit for a client move; an M21 that has all the reliability of the AK-47 but with superior 5.56mm ammunition and a 30-round magazine, Glock-17, 9mm pistol—not pretty but totally reliable, 22 covert pistol with a 6-round magazine, Minimi 5.56 mm belt-fed light machine gun 1000 rounds a minute, range about 800 yards, B4 Body Amour/ Tactical Vest, Kevlar helmet, smoke grenades, yellow are best—it looks just like gas, it is totally harmless but still has the desired effect if you need to create some space quickly, emergency medical trauma pack, maps and GPS. More phones and radios than British Telecom, flashlight and a pocket for your Rolos. © A. Boyd

Simple Flat Bread Pizza

Serves around 5–6 persons (... or 3 normal-sized Royal Marines)

This is a great dish for coming back into camp after a hard day and looking for a quick and easy meal to share with your team and kick back and relax. Add a cold beer to accompany the dish and for a moment you will forget where you are. This dish is also great the next day cold and can be taken on the road as any addition to your rations, under your next mission.

INGREDIENTS:
5–6x flatbread, pitta type
2x finely chopped onions
1x tin chopped tomatoes
Tomato puree
TOPPINGS OF CHOICE:
Grated cheese (P-for plenty)
Mashed tuna flakes
Chopped peppers (green/red)
Sliced alternative sausage (chicken/beef)
Cooked & shredded chicken pieces
Sliced mushrooms

METHOD:

Preheat an oven to gas-mark 8

Take the pitta flatbreads and lay them out on a baking tray. Add a liberal amount of tomato puree to each of the flatbread and spread evenly across the bread to the edges. Drain the tin of tomatoes into a bowl and mash to a chunky consistency and spread evenly on each of the flat bread tops.

Now add your choice of toppings as you prefer, i.e., cheese/onion/mushroom — or — tuna flakes — or — peppers/sausage/onion — to your own creative preference.

Bake in the oven for approximately 15–20 minutes until the base is a medium golden-brown colour. Once cooked through, place the hot pizza to one side and allow for cooling before serving.

Additional after-cooking ideas could be to add: light soy sauce to taste, or salsa, or coleslaw. Serve with fresh salad and enjoy.

A great meal to eat hot or saved for later to be taken as part of a pit-stop snack.

Bandit Country

BEN — *AKA, The Boxing Jock*

- *Former*: Sergeant in the Argyle and Southern Highlanders.
- *Active service*: Northern Ireland, Afghanistan, Iraq and Cumbernauld.
- *Security:* Six years a security professional in Iraq. SIA Qualified, Outstanding Team Leader.
- *Additional*: Never buys the coffee. Direct descendent of Hamish McScrooge.

At the height of the troubles in Northern Ireland, South Armagh and in particular the area around Crossmaglen, was known as Bandit Country. The British Army learnt a healthy respect for the IRA's ability to plan and execute effective strikes agents their bases and foot patrols. The object of patrolling on foot is to dominate the ground and deny the enemy the ability to move freely; this is the British Army's primary tactic in almost any conflict. Effectively patrolling in a hostile environment takes a high level of skill and coordination. There were SAS teams hiding in bushes, thousands of soldiers with helicopter support and the RUC all working around the clock, but the IRA's Active Service Units (ASUs) were still somehow slipping through our fingers. This was a dangerous time in a dangerous place.

I was responsible for planning and leading many of the Bandit Country patrols. He was an Argyle and part of the Scottish Regiment with a proud and historic legacy dating back to the Napoleonic Wars in France and the famous stand of the Thin Red Line at Balaclava.

By any other comparison this was a filthy war steeped in politics, bigotry and religious divide. There were no uniforms, no codes of conduct and no exclusion zones. Murder gangs operated with impunity even dictating their own terms and conditions on television, their faces hidden behind a black ski mask. Death lurked in every hedgerow, every abandoned vehicle, every culvert under the road. Thousands had been murdered in an endless war that produced only victims and no victories.

A huge yellow ball hung in the sky bathing a romantically beautiful countryside in warm, soft, liquid light. In the small town below, the chapel bells called the faithful to payer.

Inside the patrol base, my team were getting ready for this morning's task, which was to set up a vehicle checkpoint on one of the approach roads to the town. Soldiers dressed in dark camouflage loaded down with their kit climbed into the four waiting Land Rovers. I called my team together into a tight round huddle for a last set of confirmatory instructions, ending as always with, "Does anyone have any questions?"

"Ah just one question please Sergeant, will we be back in time for the game?"

The game was the big local derby between Glasgow Rangers and Celtic. The two teams were neck and neck at the top of the Scottish Football Premier League and it promised to be the action-packed highlight of the season thriller. My soldiers were split almost fifty-fifty: half Celtic fans, the other half Rangers fans and the banter had already started. Mostly the banter was light-hearted and in good humour but occasionally, especially this close to a big game, the verbal sniping could become vicious and bigoted along the same divides as the people here in Northern Ireland. It was ironic that the bigots had managed to spread their disease even into the tight-knit loyal brotherhood of the British Army.

After leaving the base, the four vehicles, each spaced about a hundred yards apart, made their way slowly around the outskirts of the town. On the pavement waiting to cross the road stood a young lady approximately in her early twenties. She was tall and slim with long silky black hair pulled off her face with a soft broad band; her huge brown eyes were a total contrast to her clear white skin. The tailgate Romeo named Billy was seated in the last vehicle. He took this hand off his rifle and gave her a little wave. The woman's expression never changed and she made no acknowledgement of the gesture.

"Ah, I think you've lost your touch Billy," came a response inside the vehicle. "I wonder what lucky bastard woke up beside her this morning."

Sitting by her feet as she crossed the road was a small black Labrador with a little teddy bear face and a pink collar.

"Nah! she's just playing hard to get, they all love the tartan torpedo." Everyone smiled at Billy's regain after his embarrassment at being 'dinged' by the girl's cold response.

"OK you lot switch on," came my call from up-front. "Three hundred yards around the next corner we will set the VCP (Vehicle Check Point)."

The four Land Rovers slowed and went into their practised procedure. They parked the vehicles at angles both left and right at the sides of the road. The concept being to slow and control the traffic through the middle, giving the patrol the ability to stop, question and search the occupants of any vehicles that looked suspicious.

Anyone already known to the security services was automatically stopped and their details passed by radio back to the operations centre for verification. Even if the details are reported back to be that of a known player, soldiers have the capacity to hold the suspect for as long as is possible while operations or ground teams determine the next courses of action. Experienced IRA men will just play along, they will answer soldiers' questions, be reasonably polite and give you no reason, or excuse to do anything other than let them go. Some will even start a friendly likeable banter with you; it's almost like a Jedi mind trick if you fall for it. Soldiers remember that they were up against stone-cold killers, who thought little in regard to the death and destruction they dealt in. So the stopping and checking of a vehicle was of little consequence to the experienced IRA man.

As time wore on, the team were getting restless and constantly checked on the time, shaking their heads and looking at me. The big game would start in just over an hour and it would take at least that long to get back to base.

There was a break in the traffic and finally I said, "OK collapse the VCP and let's get out of here!"

In seconds, the vehicles were pointing in the right direction and we were off. No scenic route on the way back, just directly through the town up the winding hill and back into camp.

Once we were back in the camp, I watched as they walked towards the unloading barrels. Instinct told me something was wrong.

"Monty, where is Billy?" I asked.

"Isn't he with you?"

The world suddenly fell out of my arse. I could feel my heart race and the blood in my veins ran cold as I realised someone was missing. A few years earlier, three young Scottish soldiers had gone missing— two of them were brothers. They had been captured whilst off duty by the IRA and shot dead in Belfast. The life expectancy of a separated soldier in Bandit Country wasn't good.

"Load up now!" I ordered. There was no time to waste and every minute counted. If he was discovered on his own then his life was over and probably in the most gruesome way imaginable. The four Land Rovers sped back down the hill, hardly slowing for the bends. The oncoming Sunday after-church traffic was being pushed left and right as the four vehicles stormed down the white line in the centre of the road.

Then… there he was, walking down the middle of the road waving his arms and shouting instructions to imaginary soldiers in the fields on either side of him, "OK you lot move up on the right, that's far enough just go firm there!" followed by, "Push forward you lot on the left!" I didn't know whether to punch him or kiss him. "Where the hell did you get to, you Muppet?"

"I went for a quick pee in the field and when I looked up you were all driving off down the road."

"What's that?" I asked pointing to the ground. On a string by Billy's feet was a black Labrador with a pink collar.

"Oh! that's my search dog," Billy replied, "she's been great, she played along with the whole thing like a true professional."

We quickly reloaded into the vehicles and went off at speed. Back in camp and with much dismay by the rest of the squad, they were by now showing the highlights of the big game that had ended 0-0, not a single goal after ninety minutes of football.

My Jocks made the little Labrador a bed from a cut down repack box and an old army blanket. She had a liking for ration pack biscuits which came as no surprise to anyone since they have all the resemblance to dog biscuits anyway. I then took a closer look at the dog's collar.

"Hello Pippa, I think I know who you are."

On the back of Pippa's dog-tag was a phone number and an hour later, the same beautiful young lady we had seen earlier arrived at the guardroom. She was wearing light blue jeans and a white lamb's wool top that stopped about two inches short of the waistband on her jeans. She wore no makeup or jewellery but had an elegance that would make Cindy Crawford look about as graceful as the Frankenstein Monster. Her name was Rhea and she asked if she could speak to a soldier called Billy who had found her dog.

Billy folded his arms across his chest sighed a deep, fake breath and then explained that the dog had now been signed up as a career soldier and was already in her training. And that she now had army dog tags, an ID card with an official service number and even her own bed space here in the guardroom.

"If we let her go now, she will be posted AWOL and that is a very serious offence in the British Army ma'am."

Rhea looked worried then smiled catching on to Billy's pretending. She said thank you for finding her little dog and looking after her.

"She likes to go chasing rabbits but then gets herself lost…" said Rhea.

Two days later Billy called Rhea to ask how Pippa was and if she was still chasing rabbits. After a romance, Billy and Rhea were married the following year, and they now live happily in Edinburgh, Scotland with Sienna their beautiful baby daughter…

Billy works offshore on an oil rig in the North Sea and I dodge roadside bombs for a living in Iraq.

Ben's wee tip for life…
"Yesterday's history, tomorrows a mystery, today's a gift, that's why it's called the present."

The Basra Omelette

Serves X-number of persons as desired

A personal favourite among the drivers and escort teams for breakfast or brunch prior to starting the day's routine. In Iraq, eggs were plentiful and there was rarely any issue obtaining this much-desired ingredient. Additional contents to the dish were plentiful and creative, from leftover meals from the night before, to all manner of vegetables/cheeses. Imagination was always the key. This quick simple dish is a favourite for the guys to cook on a Friday when the cook is on his day off. The recipe differs each week as everyone insists on their own method of cooking and ingredients, which is typically defined by an argument and someone storming off swearing.

INGREDIENTS:

3x eggs per person
1x chopped onions
Whatever is in the fridge that is not out of date or a health risk.
A sprinkling of common sense (not always available)
1x quarter cup of milk
Salt and pepper to season

METHOD:

Crack 3–4 eggs into a mixing bowl and beat generously with a fork until the egg yolk and white are a golden creamy consistency. Add the milk, salt and pepper and mix thoroughly.

Meanwhile preheat a frying pan with a dollop of oil on a medium-high heat. Add in the onion (or other desired ingredients) and allow to warm through. Once ready, add the egg-mix and gently stir in the mix until the edges start to harden. Using a spatula/spoon, working from the outside of the pan in towards the middle, pull the egg-mix towards the centre of the pan, this will create a fluffy texture for the omelette. Repeat this process working your way around the full circumference of the pan until the egg-mix has moved from a runny consistency to a firm texture. Flip the omelette fully over and cook through until the ingredients are a golden-brown colour. Once completed, allow the mix to settle and remove from the heat.

For best results — place the pan under a preheated oven grill and grill the dish until colour is a golden brown.

A Moment on the Lips

DAZ

- *Former*: Royal Marines SNCO, Hovercraft Pilot and Ships Diver.
- *Saw active service in*: Far East, Northern Ireland.
- *Security:* Sixteen years a security professional in Afghanistan, Lebanon, Yemen, Jordan, Oman and Iraq.
- *Additional*: Security Manager and professional operations guru and possesses true Commando spirit and ethos. A really bad dancer.

If you ever found yourself in Basra (southern Iraq) as an operator/team leader/manager/street musician then you were in for a treat. Basra is many things to many people; it is an enigma of sorts, it is frustrating, it is infuriating, it is undefining. It is full of history and there are actual moments of beauty to confuse the unsuspecting and ready to make you even more frustrated than you were before. Its people are a giant melting pot of tradition, religion and modern thinking. They are historical yet they see what they want for themselves as a future; they are incredibly courteous, smiling politely, yet they are willing to run you over if it benefits them. It was this melting pot of an enigma that drew me in some years ago and has kept me here all these years. Below is a typical meal-time extravaganza and my new comedy entertainment, enjoy.

Finding the Cook:

The first obstacle is physically getting into the kitchen. This depends on who has the key to the door, which presumably would be the cook. However, most Fridays finding the cook is the first challenge, as he does not always sleep in his room. This can take half an hour, as he religiously turns his phone off to avoid being called relentlessly to ask where he is. The cook is from Pakistan, as are a number of the small team of Pakistanis who live on camp. They all have their own rooms but share a propensity to randomly migrate around the camp, taking turns in having sleepovers in each other's room, so it's anyone's guess where they will be. Occasionally they attempt to outsmart the expats by hiding in the Bangladeshi quarter.

On locating the cook, the primary issue is physically locating the keys, which are not always with him. The keys are sometimes with the Iranian lads who like to cook for themselves on a Thursday night. Locating the keys can take a further 15-30 mins, depending on how many times they have passed hands. This is arguably the fun part particularly in the summer when the temperature starts creeping towards 50 degrees Celsius by eleven a.m.

When the keys are finally found, the next phase is to inspect the fridge and larder. The fridges are not the pinnacle of hygiene that one would expect and it takes a certain type of person to rummage around a fridge in Basra. As does a trip into the walk-in larder, which anyone who doesn't have a strong gag reflex is advised to avoid. Each week without fail, there is a requirement to go to the shop to buy a missing ingredient. Typically, eggs. This leads into the next phase which can be the most frustrating because it involves support from a local.

Buying the Ingredients:

The shop is 200m from the camp, but due to the threat environment and a series of historic deeds of stupidity, none of the expats, i.e., the non-Iraqis are permitted to walk the short distance. We now proceed into the first opportunity to lose our temper for the day, which is typically generated from a short conversation with the duty watchkeeper. It starts with the age-old question: "Can I please get the ops driver to take me to the shop? I only need some eggs. I'll be two minutes."

"No, he is tired," comes the reply.

"OK, I respect that he is tired but it's only eleven a.m. and he hasn't left the camp once today and he is the duty ops driver."

"OK. I will call him and ask this as a favour." Minutes pass by and then, "... OK, I spoke with him. He wants to go after prayers. This is better for him."

"Prayers are at twelve thirty, that is ninety minutes away and I want to cook for the lads who are hungry."

"I will call him again and tell him."

We now sit in limbo, awkwardly waiting in the Ops Room, for anywhere between 15-30 mins for the duty ops driver to arrive, which I should add is somewhat irritating as his room is in the adjacent portacabin, less than ten metres away. However, being culturally sensitive and polite, the advisable course of action is to pretend you are so genuinely glad that he has taken his time to slip on his shoes and stagger into the Ops Room. Point to note, one must allow a further 10-15 minutes for handshaking and pleasantries prior to a vehicle being selected. And he must drink a cup of sweet black tea to recharge his batteries from the arduous 10m walk. This is completely understandable…

As with any task, the ops driver must ask, because they are trained in secret to ask a series of intellectually draining myopic questions:

1. *Where do you want to go?*
2. *How long will you be?*
3. *Who is going?*
4. *Can this be done later?*
5. *Can we go tomorrow?*
6. *Can I go and pray first?*
7. *Will you buy me lunch/cigarettes/a gift?*

Response

1. To the shop—the watchkeeper has explained this. So did I… twice.

2. About two minutes—I just need to grab some eggs, nothing else.

3. Just the two of us. Or maybe one of the other lads... OK, three of us, as one of the Ugandan lads needs a phone card. So in terms of question 2, please change that to 5 minutes in the shop max.

4. No mate, we are all hungry.

5. No, definitely no. Would really like to go now please.

6. If we leave now, you will be back in time for Friday prayers. As you shouldn't be needed for the rest of the day. It's Friday.

7. No fags, but I will buy you some biscuits. They are a gift.

Now at this point, the watchkeeper usually steps in with the most dangerous aspect of the recipe, which is, to use his own initiative. This now puts all the expats in the Ops Room on edge. It always unequivocally starts with the same chilling phrase:

"I think it's much better if..."

a) You go tomorrow.

b) The mechanic takes you in his vehicle. I can call him now.

c) You ask the cook to find some eggs.

d) You send the cook—he knows how to buy eggs.

e) You go after prayers.

f) I can drive and the ops driver can manage ops for an hour. I know a better place in the city for eggs, near my house an hour away.

Response

a) No. Fer fucks sake, no! I want to go now.

b) No, the mechanic isn't even on camp. Look at the CCTV—he's gone. Did he even come in today?

c) The cook is on his day off. And we have checked the kitchen. There are no eggs. Trust me, seven of us looked.

d) The cook is on his day off.

e) Nope, prayers are in an hour. Fer fucks sake, can we just go now? Please.

f) That's not a great idea — is it? — he doesn't speak English or understand how to manage the Ops Room.

If you still have the will to live or the appetite for the next phase, then you proceed to the gameshow activity, that is, finding the ops pickup truck. One could be forgiven for thinking the pickup outside the ops room is the allocated vehicle. Many a foolish man has fallen for this ostensible common-sense approach. The ops pickup is determined by whichever set of keys the watchkeeper hands over, as by now, he is pissed off at being rebuffed at his offering to coordinate the epic voyage to the shop. The ops pickup can be in any one of the random hidey holes on camp, but never the garage carpark, as that would be far too easy and predictable. Notably, this is the second time that common sense is rejected, as vital ingredients of the recipe. On locating the ops pickup, you must then proceed to a heated yet brief argument that the driver needs money to fuel the truck up, as he needs 30 dollars to top up for the 400m total round trip, despite the truck fuel tank being half-full... not half-empty.

The next step is reasonably simple, the drive to out of camp to the shop. Leaving camp involves shaking hands and the occasional awkward kiss, with everyone lingering around the gate, apart from the gate sentry, as he is sleeping in his room. However, it is fortunate that all the guys lingering around the gate are the off-duty sentries, as they cannot sleep any more as they slept when they were on duty. Once free of the mass send-off, you are faced with a very quick yet often life-changing experience of a Basra road. It would be too stereotypical to depict a scene of goats on the road herded by young shepherds, small motorbikes with three or four passengers balanced on the back, wild dogs jogging down the road with the tongues hanging out of their dry mouths, or even a full burka-clad widow shaking her hands at the sky wailing and shouting as a form of begging. But alas, I fear that is exactly what you will see in the brief route to the shop. Try to avoid momentary depression.

On arrival at the shop, with the proviso that you have not crashed or been stopped by the police looking for a kickback, you will be greeted by six to ten grubby browned-eyed kids in thick woolly jumpers, irrespective of the weather. They want to sell you tissues or some other random shit that you don't actually need, such as warm chewing gum. So, you will have to fend them off and head into the relative calm and cool sanctuary of the shop with its dubious musty smell. The shop is a bright vista of shit, mainly from China and Iran, foodstuffs that will make your stomach knot and much randomness on sale, like an exercise bike, or a set of skis or a wedding dress.

Greetings need to be exchanged with the owner who usually shouts, "Manchester United, good, good!" with his thumbs in the air. The eggs are typically found at the right side of the shop next to the containers of nuts, all under the watchful gaze of a young teenage boy glued to the TV, grazing bare-handed in the nuts. He will laboriously handover a tray of greyish-brownish eggs, which are far from appealing and nothing more than appetite suppressants. You must then do a lap of the shop, to feed one's curiosity to see if there is actually anything in there worth buying. Finally, its back to the pickup and through the scrum of mucky orphans whilst laden with: the eggs, shower gel and a plastic plant from China with massive pink leaves.

The trip back to camp should be relatively brief and you must insist that the driver, who by now is so seriously fatigued that he can hardly keep his eyes open, must not deliberately run over any of the pack of wild manky dogs living outside the camp gates. Getting back into camp involves the complete reverse cycle of handshaking and the reuniting of old friends from fifteen minutes ago. However, this time, you will have to show them the entire contents of your shopping bag. It is guaranteed that someone will ask for the pink plastic plant as a gift. Depending on how tired and fed up you are hinges on whether you keep the plant or not. However, it would serve as a token to create a lifelong friendship with Abdullah, who proclaims he has never seen a thing of such beauty. Despite the fact that there are several similar plastic plants at the front gate, but none of them are his. With the plant handed over and the shower gel reluctantly given to the driver as his gift for his friendship and support during the epic journey, you can now proceed to the kitchen.

Cooking:

The first step is to find the master switch to turn the electricity on and get the air conditioning running. Once the antiquated AC is rumbling and spitting water everywhere, you will need someone to turn on the gas, which is in beaten rusty old gas bottles outside. Now this stage is a lottery and takes two people and a good set of ears. The bottles outside are somewhat muddled in order and do not necessarily correspond to the appliance on the other side of the wall. Therefore, one person turns the gas on and the second listens for a hiss. Do not use a lit rolled-up newspaper as the cook does as he swings it under all the gas rings, this may cause you to lose an eyebrow or fringe, or both.

Gas on. Finally:

It is usually at this stage that someone with infinite wisdom and enthusiasm enters the kitchen and issues their sage advice on how to prepare an omelette. Just give him some festering onions and a handful of warm squishy tomatoes to chop. Task a third person to find some plates and give them a wash. Take the eggs, approximately 3x per person and crack them into a battered metal dish and whisk. Season if you like, using a dusty container off the larder shelf with Arabic writing on, which maybe be salt or pepper or Chernobyl strength chilli powder. Whatever you take off the shelf, check inside for cockroaches before adding to the eggs. Fry off the onions and tomatoes in some brownish oil and add the eggs, stirring occasionally. Cook until firm. Or until you are satisfied nothing in the pan is going to kill you… or render you toilet bound, for the proceeding 48 hours. WhatsApp all the guys letting them know that some food is ready and brace yourself for the stampeding feet coming through the kitchen door. Serve on a plate(s). Sit in the warmth of a 40°C dining area and enjoy your omelette. Leave the dishes for the lads to do and make a silent vow to buy several packets of noodles during the week, in order to avoid that whole travesty again next Friday.

Convoy All-Day Breakfast Roll

Serves 4–6 big lads with appetites.

Convoy missions were long, arduous and always time-consuming. Eating was always a luxury under constant time and task constraints. This ready-made dish was served as an 'anytime' meal for teams on the go and could be eaten as desired. It is both filling and tasty.

INGREDIENTS:
6x Iraqi samoon (flat pitta-type bread)
18oz alternative sausages
6x eggs
6x fresh tomatoes

6oz mushrooms
1x chopped onion
Olive oil
Butter/margarine
Brown sauce
Worcestershire sauce
Salt & pepper

METHOD:

On a gas ring with medium-high heat, add a small dollop of olive oil to a frying pan and allow to warm through. Add the sausages and cook through. Once cooked, remove from the pan and move to a side plate.

Without cleaning the frying pan, place back on a heat and add a fresh dollop of olive oil and now add onions and mushrooms and season with salt and pepper. When the onions become transparent, add a healthy splash of Worcestershire sauce and simmer for 1–2 minutes stirring regularly. Now re-add the sausages to the frying pan and cook through, allowing the sausages to coat with seasoning and sauce. When fully coated, reduce the heat and allow to simmer for 2–3 minutes before removing and adding to a side plate.

With the frying pan back on the heat, add another dollop of olive oil and bring up to a medium heat and add eggs for frying. Fry the eggs according to personal preference or choice. While eggs are cooking, thinly cut the tomatoes and warm through the pitta bread (samoon) either in a toaster, or close to the gas fire without burning. Remove the mix from the heat.

Open the bread by using a sharp knife cutting the samoon down along the seam and spread butter/margarine inside. Now add slices of tomato, sausages, mushroom, onion and fried egg. Season further with salt and pepper to taste and add brown sauce as desired. Serve with a large mug of tea and enjoy.

The Gift That Keeps On Coming

ROBBIE

- *Former*: Royal Marines JNCO, Security Professional.
- *Saw Active Service*: Northern Ireland, Norway, the Gulf on 'Operation Safe Haven'.
- *Security:* SIA Security and Advanced Security Management.
- *Additional*: Happiest when someone else is cooking.

Convoy Escort Team (CET) leaving Baghdad Airport on yet another escort duty through hostile territory. © R. Stevenson

In 2009, we were at the height of militant activity in Iraq and there were no signs of any let-up. There was no doubt that Iraq, at that time, was arguably *the* most dangerous country on the planet; the most bombed, the most shot up, the most booby-trapped location on the globe and we three rascals (Alan, Scotty and I) were right in the middle of it. There had been a steady increase of attacks on private security teams leading up to that 2009 period, which had seen multiple casualties among security contractors and military alike: a rocket/mortar/IED does not differentiate what or who it strikes, it only knows maiming, injury or death. Every journey, every mission was fraught with danger and a chance to get spanked by any one of the long list of methods of attack, incorporated by any one of the many militant groups that operated throughout the country. It was a constant running of the gauntlet every time we stepped outside the wire and never a question of *if* we would get hit, more of *when* we'd get hit.

At home, at this time, Iraq had become old news and the world rarely made mention of it unless something enormous happened. We were still two years away from the allied forces' handover to the Iraqi people and five years from the savage ISIS insurgency, but in this moment, we had problems of our own to deal with and that involved armed militants striking at any targets of foreign interest, military or security.

One day, during the summer that year, we received word that our client wanted to travel from our camp in

Basra to FOB Warhorse, which was a US military camp to the north of Baghdad, close to the city of Baquba. Our client had previously built the camp for the military and was now providing life support to the men and women who lived and worked inside it. The only issue was that we were in Basra and about as far south from Baghdad as you could likely get yet still remain inside the country. This meant a long journey, over 600km with several hours of pure driving along some of Iraq's most notorious and deadliest roads.

As a Team Leader, I considered myself incredibly lucky to have both Al and Scotty with me. Not only were they my closest friends but the only lads I wanted with me especially if we were heading into something nasty. Both of them were Team Leaders in their own rights and bloody good ones at that, but when we worked together Al & Scotty were happy for me to take the lead. Neither of them liked the constant, enormous amount of paperwork involved with running a team and I didn't mind it so much. It was a system that worked well for us three, but at any time either one of them could step up and take over. What made us so effective was that having worked so long together, we thought as one unit, acted as one and *just did* what needed to get done with no arguments, no fuss and no bother. For me as a leader that was the solid foundation I needed, because if we ever got into trouble, I would need to focus on my job of leading the team and not worry about other lesser problems, as both Alan and Scotty had it covered and would already be dealing with the issue, taking the pressure off me.

Scotty was out on R&R which left Alan and I to plan and prep for the mission, so we both got busy with our maps and planned our primary, secondary and even back-up routes. We identified fall-back locations and emergency camps. We prepped all the stores and ammunition we would need to take for this trip, grabbing extra ammo, extra medical kit, extra batteries, food, water and spares for the vehicles. We checked radios, mobile phones and Thuryah satellite phones. We went through a tried and tested system of planning, prepping and leaving nothing to chance.

We got our trusted and experienced team of Iraqis busy. They had been with us for a number of years and ran missions like this as second nature to them. They emptied their magazines before cleaning them and replenishing them. Weapons were stripped, checked, cleaned and oiled. In addition to personal weapons, we would be taking the Minimi belt-fed section support machine gun with us as a much-needed back-up, so this too was stripped and cleaned as well. I ensured all my official Iraq paperwork was available and close at hand (and there was much of it, nearly a full inch of authority papers which would allow us to travel) as we would be going through many, many checkpoints so I needed to ensure that they were ready to show to any police officers and quickly. We didn't trust the Iraqi Police; their corruption was well known, as were their sympathies to the militia, but to move around Iraq we had little choice other than to go through their CPs. Our Iraqis washed and cleaned the vehicles, checked fluids, oils and lubricants. They ensured we had all the stores packed away, as well as all the breakdown gear we'd need. If we broke down, we'd need a quick and simple solution to get out of any situation, so tow-ropes, shackles and spare tyres were all inspected and packed away carefully. We prepped all of our individual overnight gear as well, as we'd be staying in Baghdad a couple of nights so took everything we would need. In the end, and with everything ready, I had no reason to think we couldn't cope with whatever might be thrown up at us. We were all old hands in Iraq; we knew the lay of the land, its people and its dangers so I was happy that our planning covered as much as we could humanly foresee. We all knew that there was always the *unforeseen* element, but I was confident enough that we could deal with that on the hoof, as long as we stayed frosty and alert.

The following morning, we were up and, after a check-in with the Operations Room, we set off. Oddly enough, the trip to Baghdad was uneventful and we made the capital in good time. We pulled into Victor-2, our main company HQ, just after midday and Alan got to work refuelling the vehicles, whilst I checked us in with the Baghdad Ops team. We still had over an hour to go and so with bodies stretched, refreshed and bladders emptied, we set off again.

We arrived at the gates of FOB Warhorse sometime after one p.m. and we escorted our clients inside the camp to their meetings. Ensuring that the protection team were in place for our clients, Alan took the vehicles further around to the second northerly car park as the camp had a one-way system, meaning our clients would come out the second exit point of the camp and I joined him there. The carpark was just a dry and dusty square patch of land outside the top left corner of the camp, roughly the size of a football pitch. It was flat with only a line of 4ft-high concrete blast walls, roughly a foot thick, all in a single line to denote a central lane marking for exiting light/heavy traffic.

With the vehicles parked ready to go and a check-in with the protection team, I walked back towards the main road, as this was the only place I could get a clear signal for my mobile phone and outside the ECM radio-jamming bubble. I then called in to HQ with a sitrep (situational report) and reported all was well.

No sooner had I parted with our situation than there was an almighty explosion to our front approximately 100m away on southern edge of the carpark. The noise was loud and deafening and for a moment I was stunned, like a rabbit caught in headlights as plumes of smoke, dust and debris were thrown high into the air. In less than a heartbeat, I suddenly caught hold of myself and ducked behind one of the short concrete blast walls that ran towards the rear exit of the camp. It wasn't much but it was the best I had under the circumstances.

A second explosion was followed by a third and a fourth as I realised that whoever was firing these mortars were now walking them in towards us. Whether we were the intended target or the US army camp was, remains unknown but one thing for sure was the explosions were getting closer to where we were, putting us in a precarious situation.

After the fourth explosion, I saw Alan run towards me, keeping low along the line of blast walls. He had been near me when the first explosion happened and had run back to shout at the team to lie flat, and against the only cover we had available, our armoured cars. There was no chance of getting into the camp; the military had that locked up the moment the first round landed, so we were stuck outside with nowhere to go and no choice but to rough it out. *Boom... Boom... Boom!* they went, edging ever closer; seven, eight, nine I counted as Alan waited and then, like a county court judge legging it from a house of ill repute when the peelers came knocking, he was up and off again. Suddenly a mortar round landed just 60 metres away and my blast wall wobbled violently in its aftershock; the air seemed to vanish and I was covered in all kinds of dusty shite. I watched as Alan lost his footing, stumbled slightly and for a second, I thought the worst, but he then up-righted himself and ran hell for leather to where I was. I smiled as I saw this breathless lump of a man come bounding in. In truth I was fucking glad to see him and if this was going to be the end, then there was no one else I'd rather be with right then.

"You losing it in your old age grandad!" I called out to him still smiling like a loon.

"Feck off," he shouted back. "I've still plenty left in this tank," and he smiled back as we hunkered down even lower behind the wall as the next round landed.

They were now so close and so loud that my ears popped and everything muffled as if I were underwater. My body jarred and tightened as if all my muscles were suddenly pulled taught like guitar strings. We braced ourselves for what was surely to come next. Here we were in the middle of Iraq, in the middle of a giant, flat dry and dusty patch of land, thousands of miles away from home and hiding behind a few feet of concrete. I suddenly started laughing uncontrollably and when Alan saw me, he smiled back—most likely *at* me rather than with me. That surreal moment to our situation was just hilarious; there was no glory coming, no gun-blazing final stand Alamo style, just two blokes in the dirt, in the middle of nowhere and with a mortar round about to land on their heads. Typical!

There was a long excruciating pause… an eerie lengthy silence, as the echoes of the last explosion bounced off buildings and trees drifting away into the distance. I heard nothing except the high-pitched whine in my ear. I wanted the whole thing to be over, and in my head, called out, *C'mon damn you, just get it over with!* but nothing came. An excruciating age passed and slowly, very slowly, I looked up. What I saw was even funnier as I saw Alan looking as if someone had tipped a big bag of brown flour over him, for he was covered head to foot in dust, rock and bits of debris. He laughed back at me seeing the same I reckon. Then as suddenly as it had started, it was over. The mortar round that we had both expected to drop on us never came and we both blew out a long breath of relief.

After checking that the clients and the protection team were OK, we sorted ourselves out. I called Baghdad and reported the events while Alan readied the team once again. Thank God no one was hurt: ten rounds of mortars and nothing to show for it but some dusty dirty fellas. Eventually the back gate opened and out came the team with our clients, shaken but otherwise all OK. After bundling them in the vehicles, we set off for Baghdad once again.

The next morning washed and fresh, we headed back to Basra arriving sometime after lunch. After de-kitting and sorting the vehicles, weapons and kit out we headed back to our team room. I had just started typing up the mission report when a half-naked Alan appeared wrapped in a towel that might as well been a tea-towel for all of its size.

"Rob, can you take a look at this for me?"

I looked at him sceptically. "I think I've been stung by something."

He lifted his arm and I saw a small red welt about a half inch in diameter just below his armpit, which was sitting on a fist-sized bruise.

"Hmmm," says I, "right go lie down over there and let me take a closer look." On closer inspection I saw what I thought was the barbed tail of a bee, just barely sticking out from the centre of the welt. I quickly grabbed my med kit and took out my tweezers and then, gently grabbing the tail, I pulled. Alan gave a slight grunt and then said nothing else. I twisted and gently pulled harder and with some effort I saw movement and with a final tug it freed. I was surprised to see not the barbed tail from an insect, but a piece of green-and-white metal, about the size of a thumb nail. It was a piece of shrapnel from one of the mortar detonations which must have clipped Alan, possibly when he had stumbled in the carpark. His ribcage had saved his life, the shrapnel had come in over the top of his assault vest, hit his rib and embedded itself just under the skin. He had then travelled with this piece of metal all the way back from Baquba to Basra without so much as a complaint. I cleaned and dressed his wound and if I hadn't already been in awe of the man, I was now even more so. Alan and I made many more trips in Iraq of a similar nature and each in turn carried its own amazing story, but that's for another time and one for over a beer or two.

Robbie's personal security tip… *"When someone is looking for volunteers, always walk around with a hammer; if anyone sees you they will naturally assume you already have a job and will select someone else for the task."*

MEMORIES FROM IRAQ 02:

(2009) A short water break on Iraq's notorious MSR Tampa, somewhere south of Baghdad as we head south to Basra. Unbeknown to either of us at this time was that Alan was carrying a piece of shrapnel embedded under his left arm after being hit by a mortar attack the day before. It wasn't until we reached Basra that we managed to get it out of him and realised he'd carried it some 700 kms. © R. Stevenson

MEMORIES FROM IRAQ 02:

(2010) Alan in a reflective mood, inside Saddam Hussein's Tikrit Palace. We were returning from Kirkuk on a four-day mission and on our way back to Baghdad when we called in to the palace for an overnight layover. It was said that the lake behind was manmade and had been built for Saddam Hussein to enjoy his favourite water sports. © R. Stevenson

The Contractors Curry

This is an authentic and easy little dish from both my summer and winter collections. It is a tasty treat but its real beauty is its simplicity to create. In today's fast-paced work environments, fast and convenience foods fill the gap, leading to obesity and laziness. Here I hope to show you a quick and reasonably cheap alternative that will impress both friends and family alike. A rapid, robust receptacle of good wholesome nourishment, with a taste of the Asian exotic.

Another important feature of this dish is that it confirms to those who consume it that their mouths and anuses, with everything in between is still in perfect working order!

YOU WILL NEED:
Two forms of mess-tin and a small portable camping gas stove. A sharpened knife or other such implement. (At this point I would like to advise that any Royal Marines should get a responsible adult to do anything involving cutting).

INGREDIENTS:
Meat, preferably chicken but literally any meat will do
Small container of cooking oil
Curry powder (P for Plenty)
Garlic, ready crushed, bought in small jar

Onion, only if practical
Chilli flakes (P for Plenty)
Coconut milk (If not sourced then I have in the past used the UHT sachets from a transport café, the older the better as this gives a yoghurt-like consistency)
Salt
Tabasco Sauce (a necessity in any Daysack)
Boil-in-the-bag rice.
Locally sourced bread, preferably something that will absorb and not snap.

METHOD:

Retrieve from your Daysack or Vehicle Storage Bin all utensils and ingredients. Light gas stove with a naked flame (Again, Royal Marines will benefit from help from a supervising adult to avoid a raging inferno). Use a small amount of the oil to bring the mess tin alive. Add curry powder and chilli flakes, season with salt and pepper and fire in Tabasco until your eyes and nose begin to run. Add meat to the mix; as stated, chicken is best for speed but any form of meat will do. If asked what meat it is then ask what the recipient likes and assure them that's what it is. Don't worry as the spices and sauces will destroy all taste buds anyway.

Once the meat is browned all over add the milk, coconut or otherwise. Stir in, adding more chilli flakes, Curry powder and Tabasco to taste. Let this simmer for approximately 10–15 mins. This is the ideal time to place a second mess tin on top containing water and the boil in the bag rice. I highly recommend Uncle Ben's!

Take the opportunity while your meal is simmering to soak in the ambience of your surroundings. Listen to the nature, converse with a loved family member or friend. Maybe even jot down some relaxing poetry.

Eventually your feast is ready to serve; once again, season to your particular taste. Then simply throw all the cooked foodstuffs into the same mess tin and enjoy!

NB. Remember these metal surfaces will be piping hot, so perhaps get a Royal Marine friend to put his socks on his hands for protection. After the meal help him back on with his footwear on the correct feet.

Memories of an Accidental Tourist

GILLY

- *Former*: Grenadier Guards.
- *Active Service*: Ulster, Cyprus, Falklands.
- *Security*: Twelve years a security professional, Iraq.
- *Additional*: Known as The Gobby Grenadier.

I worked in the hostile environment of Iraq from the beginning of 2004 until the beginning of 2016. I worked for several companies, met hundreds of people and was a participant in thousands of memories, both in mine and in those of others.

In 2007 I worked on Convoy Duties; our contribution to the war effort was essential… apparently, in that we collected waste fuel oil and dead vehicle batteries from US military camps and bases countrywide.

The fuel oil was refined (diluted), to create cooking oil and the batteries were recharged and used to power the Iraqi space programme, or milk floats or bumper cars or something else I really couldn't give a toss about. We were paid to move stuff and it didn't really matter to us what that stuff was.

Our team crewed five security vehicles, three Toyota Land Cruisers and two intimidating Reva armoured fighting vehicles. We would usually escort sixteen flatbed HGVs and a spare tractor unit, known as the Bobtail. The escorted trucks were driven by civilian contractors from various countries but predominantly African nations and India/Pakistan. Our transport was routinely maintained by company-employed former military mechanics. The maintenance of the trucks was the responsibility of the individual driver/owner. It was made clear to them upon signing their contracts that they were liable for their upkeep and ability to remain roadworthy. Any vehicle that could not be quickly repaired by the side of the road, faced destruction so as to deny the asset to the insurgents for the purpose of further terrorist acts. The preferred method of destruction was the use of a Thermite Grenade, a device that burned at over 3000 degrees and rendered the vehicle a burned-out shell, quite rapidly and impressively. For obvious reasons, this tactic was not generally used in built-up areas and the Team Leader only, usually had access to these *'Napalm Eggs'*. As an alternative to Thermite, team members also carried a stock of traditional high explosive and white phosphorous military grenades, these also did the trick, several times.

I'd like to mention at this point that that back then, as now, I have never held an HGV licence and have never driven a large truck. Although a tasking undertaken by many of the main security companies that worked in Iraq, convoy duties were far removed from the norm of Protective Security Detail employment. There were fewer of the constraints of etiquette or politeness that are normally vital for the corporate image to generate in the more customary fashion. What was important was getting the mission done and if *feelings* were hurt along the way, then so be it. With so many languages and dialects present what was necessary was a firm and robust manner, with instruction given in the most colourful of English. Missions could be brief, sometimes lasting only a day but most lasted a couple, with some stretching into a week depending upon many various factors. No mission passed without incident, ranging from the most humorous of actions to events that proved to be life-changing.

It was a stiflingly hot day in May, in my role as the Team 2i/c, I commanded the rear Reva, the tail-end Charlie. Rick, a fellow former Guardsman, was positioned in the rear turret constantly scanning our six o'clock for threats. I was sitting next to the driver, an Iraqi, as the majority of our team were, in accordance with Iraqi employment laws governing foreign security companies. There was no escape from the imposing heat; the outside temperature was probably in the forties but the effect of sitting virtually on top of the engine manifold within the wagon, pushed the inside temperature to nearer 60°C. Add to that my body armour and a flame-retardant Nomex flight suit, meant the body was squeezed of moisture in an effective weight-loss plan.

I remember being alerted over the radio, via my earpiece literally swimming within the sweat pool of my left ear. The spare Bobtail had pulled to the right and had become stationary. Cal, the Team Leader was instructing me to sort it. Only fifteen or so minutes earlier, we had crossed the city limits and entered Baghdad from the north and now faced the most testing period of a mission: transiting a hostile city and the even more hostile inhabitants whilst negotiating all manner of obstacles to reach our base back at the airport. Cal had slowed the convoy from his position up at the front in the first Reva behind a Land Cruiser acting as our Scout. This tactic was intended to buy me more time to deal with the incident without allowing me to be separated with a large gap appearing.

I ran to the driver who was by now running around in circles in his manjamas and wailing like a banshee. A quick translation saw me establish that he was informing me that some mechanical fault had caused his engine to cease functioning and that he didn't have the experience nor skill to get the said unit up and running again. Please assist me you jolly fine English fellow as you are my only hope.

Rick, in the meantime, had halted the civilian traffic to our rear. There was never time for explanations to angry commuters, so pointing the PKM Soviet machine gun in that direction, tended to cut through linguistically challenging barriers.

I jumped up into the cab and was immediately hit with an almost overwhelming stench of vile human existence that remained with me for some time. Though not as long as the stink on my gloves after I'd touched his seat, which was almost sponge like in its ability to retain the aromatic smell of his sweaty arse crack. I wanted to frag the cab immediately purely out of spite but I realised that with us already being in the city this wasn't an option. I relayed up to Cal that I was going to deny the asset by *'other means'*, though I hadn't completely decided what they would be just yet. I called one of our rear-positioned Land Cruisers to me, bundled the driver in and told our guys to get him away and double him up with another truck driver. I didn't want him to see what I was going to do to his pride and joy, not to mention his livelihood.

I shouted to Rick to pass me the 30lb lump hammer we carried as part of the vehicle kit. I was going to smash the cab, render it non-driveable and then leave it there. As I ran back to the cab I could see that the traffic had increased quite substantially in numbers and was backing up some way. Irate occupants were leaning on their horns or out of their cars and remonstrating with shaken fists and the usual inevitable finger over the throat motion. Swinging a large hammer with all the force I could muster inside the cab of an HGV wasn't too dissimilar to having a fight in a telephone box. Not the most spacious of places and a cat would soon have become bored at being swung in there and simply disappear. My first few blows destroyed the dashboard, the dials and gauges, but that was just purely aesthetical, I needed to damage it properly. I decided to concentrate my savage onslaught on the steering wheel and steering column. I aimed for the Scania in the centre and gave the rubberised logo a good thump.

Much to my bewilderment the engine burst into life…

Rick shouted down to me to stop messing about and take the keys out. The keys were out! This wasn't going to plan. Several more times I struck away totally destroying the intended targets. But, to my absolute surprise, the vehicle was not only running but was now in reverse gear, along with me in it and now heading backwards the way we had just come. To make matters worse, about three hundred-plus Iraqi car owners were getting angrier at their delay.

It was pandemonium; I was pretty much wedged into the cab to allow me room to swing; parts of the smashed cab were all around me and through the rear window, I witnessed panic unfold. The first line of motorists began to reverse into those behind them in a mad domino effect of confusion, as they too reversed back into the next line of cars and so on. All the while this plucky little Bobtail weaved and snaked its way over the road markings towards the masses and the confusion. It was like a tormented bull in the ring, getting into the stands amongst the baying crowds. I extracted myself from the cab, broken components at my feet. I looked up at Rick in the turret; he was laughing like a man possessed. Cal was calling with some urgency for a sitrep (situation report), as he needed to know what was happening.

I just didn't have the words; I knew that we needed to get away and remove ourselves from the scene with haste. Ambushes were quickly orchestrated in such circumstances of being stationary. However, I just couldn't tear my eyes away from what was unfolding before me. I composed myself and ran back to the Reva and its opened door, throwing in the hammer, only to join Rick laughing at the ridiculousness of the situation. The large, heavy door of the Reva was open with Rick perched on the end of the seating within; he too found the carnage unfolding mesmerising. In the distance we could hear the wailing sirens of the approaching Baghdad Police. I didn't relish the thought of trying to explain this in a cell over the next five years. As we drove away and re-joined the convoy, I gave a 'highlighted' version of events to Cal, knowing he would eventually enjoy my full explanation. Although he would find it hard to sound credible in his inevitable account of the incident in his Post Mission brief to our Operations Team. Looking through the reinforced Porthole on the rear door, I could clearly see the Bobtail now on top of the first white and battered saloon car, even more damage caused by having this large tractor unit crushing its roof. Still, it ploughed on, causing more chaos. Convoy Duties were never boring.

I worked with some pretty outstanding blokes and that day was so fortunate that my efforts of vehicle maintenance and traffic control had been witnessed by a colleague and confirmed as being a true reflection of what occurred. I'd have found it hard to believe if it hadn't have happened to me.

Hours later and back in the safe haven of our base camp at the airport, both Rick and I gave a detailed account of the incident to Cal, who himself kept his composure for all of about thirty seconds before finding the whole thing as hilarious as we did. I remember him asking how he was going to explain this to our higher formation. Inadvertently, we'd actually helped by staging Baghdad's first ever Monster Truck Rally, just without the Star Spangled banners… and the popcorn… or telling anyone beforehand.

Gilly's personal security tip… *"Eat and consume alcohol excessively. Fat drunks are harder to kidnap."*

Nepalese Bean Stew

This dish is both traditional and nutritious as well as being very tasty since it includes several kinds of beans. Luckily, Iraq has plenty of pulses, which are easy to obtain locally from any one of the thousands of markets dotted throughout. Time must be given for the beans to soak overnight and swell and this must be factored in when cooking this option.

INGREDIENTS:

1x cup each cups dried beans: chickpeas, soya beans, black beans, white beans, kidney beans, mung beans
500 g meat (beef/chicken) diced
1x medium onion, chopped
4-5 cloves garlic
4-5 medium tomatoes
1x Inch ginger, pulped to a paste
1 tsp fennel
Vegetable oil

SPICES:

1 tsp cumin seeds
1 tsp mustard seeds
1 tsp lovage seeds
1 tsp coriander
1 tsp powdered cumin
1 tsp turmeric powder
1 tsp red chilli powder
Salt to taste

METHOD:

Soak the beans overnight in a large bowl and allow to expand. The next day, drain the water into a separate bowl and keep to one side.

In a large pan (for slow cooking) heat a dollop of vegetable oil and add in: cumin seeds, mustard seeds, fennel and lovage seeds. Once the seeds start to pop, add in the chopped onion, garlic and ginger and cook through for another 3 minutes. Now add in the beef/chicken and fry through until the meat is light brown all over.

Once the meat is cooked through, add in the mixed beans, coriander, turmeric, chilli powder, powdered cumin and fry through all together until everything is nicely coated. Now add salt and mix again until coated and mix gently for another 3–4 minutes. Then add the tomatoes and add 4–5 cups of cool water and stir well.

Place the lid on the pan and allow to cook on a low-medium heat for 40 minutes stirring periodically and adding small amounts of water if required to prevent drying out. Allow the mixture to come back to the boil, place the lid back on and repeat stirring process periodically.

Continue to cook until the consistency reaches the desired effect — thick and soup like. Simultaneously, whilst the stew is cooking, this dish can be accompanied by cooking through some rice as a side dish or added inside the stew. For long journeys, this food can be a godsend and can easily top up a flask to stay hot whilst on the road.

Dead Men Tell no Tales

HITMAN

- *Former:* JNCO Royal Gurkha Rifles.
- *Active service*: Belize, Hong Kong, Iraq and Afghanistan.
- *Security*: Many years security professional in Iraq as a senior team leader.
- *Additional*: Don't get on his wrong side.

Contact! A roadside IED detonates prematurely as a civilian vehicle accidently triggers the device north of Baghdad. IEDs were a constant threat and widely used against security teams. They came in all shapes and sizes and many with horrific results. © R. Stevenson

It's fair to say that no one I have ever treated for more than a simple finger cut has ever survived to tell the story. Of course I say this with my tongue in my cheek, but so it was when we continued to run the gauntlet of operating in Iraq South in those early, heady days.

In 2005, working for ArmorGroup, we were running small, fast operations, moving heavily protected convoys from our base location at the Contingency Operating Base, or '*COB*' as it was more commonly known as the Basra International Airport, (or BIA). This entailed moves down to the Iraq-Kuwait border crossing point at the town of Safwan, approximately sixty kilometres to the south of the COB, to collect precious cargo trucks heading up from Kuwait. We would then meet them at the border and collect them before heading once again north to their various destinations.

In most situations, the trucks were usually a semi-armoured vehicle (if at all) and were given their own designated four-vehicle armed escort team which included a mission commander or Team Leader, a 2i/c and team of shooters. In addition to these, operations dictated that there was always a Quick Reaction Force '*QRF*' on standby, consisting of at least two armoured vehicles using the very powerful Ford Excursion within the area.

The QRFs primary task on some of these missions (dependant on cargo) was to control the road junctions, shepherd any slow-moving traffic to one side and provide additional cover in and around some of the more dangerous areas.

Today Alan was my Team Leader with me as his driver as we were running the QRF. This was the better of the two jobs, as long as you had 'eyes-on' with the convoy and voice communications, you could more or less free run and the big powerful Excursions were real boys' toys.

At that time, hostilities in the South were beginning to creep upwards numerically and continued to gather momentum, but its pinnacle was still a year or two away. Up to this point, though, we had very few issues on these trips south. The vast expanse of territory was as flat as a snooker table with views that were miles upon miles of open flat land. The three-lane highway also made things difficult for any would-be bombers and to date, only one IED had detonated along this stretch of road, so we were not expecting trouble.

Once our little convoy reached the Iraq-Kuwait border crossing, there was the usual confused four hour wait before the cargo trucks were allowed to clear customs and cross, having had all their paperwork checked and rechecked half a dozen times by bored and arrogant Iraqi border guards. We sat, hot and sweaty in the dry, dusty heat waiting patiently as the confusion of drivers, irate policemen and customs men all got into an argument over why they were being held up from being allowed to cross. Sometimes it was entertaining and other days it just bored us.

Eventually the trucks did cross, and as we checked them off as they drove by, we slipped into formation with them and headed off at speed. Driving the big heavy Excursion, I kept us close to, but not on top of, the convoy as we wound our way north, occasionally tucking in behind the last truck to allow a fast-moving car to pass or one of the big 4x4s from one of the many security companies to overtake. Some of them were really moving, as there were no speed restrictions in Iraq, no driving test, no insurance and no MOTs so it was a like the Whacky Races most days.

As we tucked in once again behind one of the container trucks, there was suddenly a loud high-velocity crack, a deafening roar and then a shockwave as the truck in front of us just disappeared in a cloud of grey/black dust, chaos and confusion. Momentarily everything went black and quiet, all in the same moment and taking only a single heartbeat, although it felt like an eternity. As suddenly as it started, the scene rushed back in a wave of utter noise, smoke and blinding debris.

Our windscreen began to *Plink Plink Plink*, as truck parts, rubber, tarmac and everything else thrown up by the explosion began raining off our glass windscreen. A wing mirror, bits of tyre and other truck debris flew in all directions amid the chaos. As I look back, I am reminded of those old, World War Two black-and-white dogfight films, where the Spitfire, having given the Messerschmitt a burst of wing cannons, then flies through the debris of the plane it had just shot up.

As the dust gave way to clarity, we could see the truck had been practically cut in two by the IED — Improvised Explosive Device — right through the main steel frame just behind the tractor unit. The trailer was broken in two from its front cab, with both exposed ends resting twisted on the road. I pulled up close beside the truck driver's door from a position about 45° to the truck, blocking traffic from coming too close.

Both Alan and I were out of our vehicle quickly and climbed up to see inside the truck cab. The first thing we saw was the driver's face, head and hands covered in blood but noted he was making a lot of noise, which is normally a good sign as opposed to silence: there was still a chance for him. I undid his seat belt and between us, we carefully lifted him down out of the cab so that he was lowered safely between the two vehicles. We climbed back into the cab to get a look at the passenger who had been sitting beside him. I remember noting how very little blood there was on him and how he was slumped back in his seat. I gently pulled him towards me and he toppled over onto the driver's seat, the back of his head was missing. *That's normally not quite a good sign,* I noted to myself. Once again, we lifted him gently down from the cab and onto the ground next to the driver; only now we saw that the truck driver was missing from the spot where he had been moments before.

There was a horrible skid of tyres behind us and we both looked up simultaneously. In his confused state, the driver had risen up and inadvertently wandered from the safety between the parked vehicles and straight into the middle of a three-lane motorway. At the same time, an SUV driver who had been heading north between the narrow gap of our vehicle and the central barrier, hadn't seen the driver wander out in front of him. He hit the driver square on, sending him some thirty feet across the road. His arms and legs spun like a rag doll before he came crashing down to a stop on the right verge of the road. We rushed over and looked down at his twisted, blood-covered body. There were no signs of life. Checking for a pulse confirmed what we suspected.

Our QRF team stayed with the destroyed truck as the main convoy continued on its way; there was no point in holding up the rest of the convoy in jeopardy so we told them to move on as we stayed with the damaged vehicle. Alan and I put the two bodies into the black rubber body bags and gently lifted them into the back of the big Ford Excursion rear. There was a moment of silence between us and there was no escaping the magnitude of what had happened. We now became automated and we held our feelings deep down as we still had a job to do and we were very exposed at this moment in time.

By now Alan and the Operations Room were on the radio; we were instructed to stay with the vehicle as long as it was safe and until the client could arrange for it to be recovered. They estimated that a recovery team could be with us in two to three hours. Alan tried to explain that there was nothing much to recover, that the truck had been cut in two by the explosion, but they were having none of it and we were still required to stay put with the broken hulk until it was recovered.

Even though we were in the middle of a flat featureless area of desert, we were already starting to draw a crowd as twenty or so local men began gathering around the truck, set fast on looting whatever was of any value. The situation would soon get out of control and we were about to get caught up in the middle of it. Almost every male in Iraq owns an AK-47 assault rifle so we were easily going to be outnumbered and outgunned. We spotted at least five or six weapons among the crowd of onlookers.

Just then the satellite phone rang. It was my good friend, big Robbie Stevenson, our operations manager.

"Al mate, is the truck on fire?" Robbie asked.

"No mate," he answered.

There was a pause on the phone followed by, "Al, is there any smoke coming from the truck?"

"No," he said again. Another pause followed by, "lads… lads! Do-you-think-it-looks-like-it's-going-to-catch-on-fire-any-time-soooon?" Robbie said slowly and deliberately.

What the fuck was he going on about? we all thought… and then slowly the penny finally dropped. He was leading us, suggesting the fact that if the vehicle was on fire, the client would determine the situation negligible and beyond recovery. We all nodded when we recognised this and our action plan suddenly became more obvious.

Al replied now with a new enthusiasm.

"Well… actually… there seems to be some smoke coming from it just now, oh! and we can see flames billowing (there weren't any)… yes the whole thing is now in flames."

"Roger that," Robbie said. "I will let the client know, get out of there and keep me updated, be safe… out!"

It was then that Al drew and cocked his pistol and put his magazine's worth of 9mm rounds through the external fuel tank from about thirty metres away. The crowd, now startled by the sound of gunfire, backed away as they fathomed what was happening. It was a small respite but for how long was anyone's guess. The expectation that the tanker would explode in a big ball of flames after the shots had passed through the thin skin, just like it did in the movies, was followed by us looking a little deflated when nothing happened. There was just a large puddle of diesel on the road, a tanker now riddled with yet more holes and locals looking rather peeved that this had just happened. Hmmmm what to do? By now the small crowd of men were becoming agitated, they quickly realised what we were trying to do and there was now low whispers and a hubbub among them, which we suspected was the men working on an opportunity to stop us and close in on the fuel.

As quickly as I could, I scrambled back inside the cab and with my knife slashed hard and fast at the seats, Al did the same on the opposite side on the passenger seat. Then collecting all the hand sanitiser (with its high alcohol content) we could find, squirted it into the exposed seat material and lit it. In just a few short minutes, the cab was ablaze with the rest of the truck and trailer soon to follow. As we watched the fire swirl out of control and the cab become consumed with fire, the local men became restless knowing that this was now a fruitless effort so began moving away. We knew this could easily change in a heartbeat if they became more agitated, so, taking the opportunity, we quickly made our exit leaving the twenty or so locals scratching their heads at the loss of free loot.

Back at the camp, the bodies were taken to the morgue and the families were notified (who would later collect the two men for local burial). We reported in to the Operations Room and wrote up our incident report. Finally, we were in a position to call it a day and Al and I went to the NAAFI for a well-deserved coffee. It had been a testing day and our nerves had held throughout the precarious and delicate situation. We knew it would not be the last time we would be tested in such a way, but for now we enjoyed the flavour of the coffee and the necessity of a small break. Tomorrow was tomorrow and no sooner had we finished our last sips of the wonderful dark aromatic coffee, than we were back in the Operations Room, planning our next mission.

***Hitman's personal security tip*…** *"Don't use the same passwords for all your devices. If compromised, it may mean you changing your dog's name."*

Chilli Jackets

Winter nights in Iraq can be perilously cold, so this dish is a must for those evenings when the weather turns sour and the team need a pick-me-up. A simple meal that will fill up the hungriest of people is just the ticket.

INGREDIENTS:

4x large potatoes (or 1 per person)
1 lb minced beef
1x red pepper (deseeded & finely chopped)
1x green pepper (deseeded & finely chopped)
1x onion (finely chopped)
400g tomatoes (chopped)
400g kidney beans
2x tbsp olive oil
2x cloves garlic
1x tbsp chilli powder
1x dollop tomato puree
250ml water
Salt & pepper for seasoning

METHOD:

After washing the potatoes clean, prick the potatoes with a fork all over. Preheat an oven to 200° degrees and allow time for the temperature to reach optimum heat. If there is access to tin/baking foil, wrap the potatoes individually; either way, place the potatoes on a tray in the middle of the oven. Check after one hour to confirm soft centre of the potato.

At the same time, heat the oil in a large frying pan and fry the onions until they turn transparent and soft. Now stir in the garlic and chilli powder and continue to stir and cook for a further 1–2 minutes.

Add in the minced beef to the frying pan and break down the mince using a fork. Continue to cook until the beef begins to brown and then add the green and red peppers, stirring continuously until they too have cooked through. Add a sprinkling of salt and pepper and mix in.

Add the tomato puree and mix in, then add the chopped tomatoes, 250ml of water and mix well. Allow the ingredients to bubble and simmer. Turn the heat down to a low-medium and allow the chilli beef to cook for approximately thirty minutes stirring occasionally. Towards the end of the thirty minutes, add in the kidney beans and mix well.

Once the potatoes have cooked through, remove them from the oven and split them in half, add a dollop of butter per potato (if desired) and ladle the cooked chilli beef over the top. Add salt and pepper as desired and serve with fresh salad and a large mug of tea.

When the team is back in and need something substantial to eat, this is a great recipe to keep the hunger pangs at bay. Copious amounts of tea go well with this dish as you settle in to those cold winter nights.

A New Sheriff in Town

TONY

- *Former:* Lance Corporal Royal Marines, fast boats coxswain.
- *Active Service:* Falkland Islands, Northern Ireland, Norway, HMS *Intrepid* and Hong Kong.
- *Additional:* Best tight-head prop in England; on a good day he made Fran Cotton look like Leonardo DiCaprio.

Fast boats and the ability to get a body of men quickly onto its target, is primarily the mainstay of Royal Marines operations. And, being a coxswain in one is nothing short of a thrill to be involved with. It's having the ability to move troops from ship to shore in the fastest possible time catching the enemy off guard or, sneaking in for silent insertion and then extracting before anyone has got wind that something is amiss. Operating in Norway at the height of winter also requires a special skill that only comes from persistent training and endless exercises in order to get it right. Along with tide-times there are: dark and light conditions, currents, waves, cloud cover, sea fog, riptides, cruise and pleasure craft to name but a few and is all part of the planning considerations that come with operations. Then there is the freezing, biting bitter Arctic cold. It's the type of cold that freezes the balls off a brass monkey and that's even after all of our issued cold-weather gear. On occasion it does have its perks though and to be honest, it is a pretty cool job to have, just look at Daniel Craig's entrance after being chosen as the next James Bond.

We had deployed to Norway one year, when another coxswain and I were volunteered for a special task. I use the word 'volunteered' loosely as no one ever volunteers for anything in the Royal Marines not without there being an ulterior motive behind it. And so it was when the Company Sergeant Major called me in one day and said, "Tony, I have a special task for you."

Here it comes, I thought to myself. But after buttering me up with details, it turned out to not be as bad as I first thought.

"No problem," says I to the Company Sergeant Major and off I went to prep the boat and dig out my best and warmest gear. Outside the temperature had dropped to minus ten and in these conditions you had less than 5–10 minutes survival time before you were a goner, so it was important that we carried all the right gear, all stowed properly and that took time. But by the time our passengers arrived, I was ready and had everything in good order, so it was just a case of running through all the boat checks before we set off.

They were a photography team from the Navy who needed some maritime steely shots of us two driving around the open sea in the fast and powerful Rigid Raiders that our Corps is famous for. It was to be a small part of the latest drive to tempt new volunteers into the Royal Marines and show them that it wasn't all about barrel-chested beasts screaming at you at some ungodly hour for having a shoelace out of place—that came later in week 6 of training, I say tongue in cheek. Our photo shoot would be putting a nice glossy finish to it and showing potential recruits that there was some glamour left in the Marines.

We quickly ran through our safety brief and he, the photographer, then went through what it was he wanted us to do. For the next few hours, we became unfashionable models as he snapped away with his camera from various positions inside the boat. Snap, snap, snap he went and I felt he was leading up to something. Eventually he asked me to take my goggles off so he could get a close-up of my face.

"Bollocks to that," I retorted. "In this weather and this icy spray, I'm likely to go blind or freeze my eyelids to my eyebrows."

My laugh was hollow, but he was dogged if nothing else. It took some persuasion, but after the offer of a couple of free pints that night (I'm so cheap) I reluctantly did as I was asked and the end result was that he got the shot he wanted. Later on, I found out that the shot had passed the scrutiny of the Royal Navy and Royal Marine recruitment team and it was then used for the latest round of advertisements — my fifteen minutes of fame, sealed once and for all.

In 1985, I found myself drafted to Hong Kong (HK) as part of maritime security support duties, working alongside the police in trying to stop illegal immigrants crossing from China into Hong Kong. As a permanent detachment of Royal Marines out there, and still being twelve years prior to the handover ceremony, it had been our job to patrol the waters around Hong Kong with stop-and-search powers with vessels attempting to enter local waters. These often ruthless, money obsessed criminals were hell-bent on smuggling people over the border for much profit and little in the way of concern or safety of their charges.

Sometimes, it was soul destroying watching as poor wretches with next to little or nothing, often with the world on their backs and bringing small children with them, try to make their way into the affluent state of Hong Kong. But HK could not sustain this financially or geographically, as there was, simply too many people already in the hustle and bustle of this small peninsula, so it needed our support to turn them about and send them back to China.

It had been a dull, fruitless day on the water in that early December, when after only a few months inside my tour I was beginning to wonder if *this* was it, what with routine patrolling, stop and searches, etc., all of which were taking its toll. I turned the Rigid Raider about after yet another slow day of much the same. Lau was on hand inside our small pursuit craft working at all the man-handling jobs, whilst I steered and powered the engines. He was a good sort, trustworthy and good humoured and we got on well as a crew and I for one was happy to have him aboard.

It was late, around 2330hrs when the radio sparked into life and I heard our callsign being hailed. It was HMS *Monkton* sat out in the bay and they called in with a possible contact heading towards the To-Lo Channel which was further around to the east of the peninsula. We were instructed to make all haste there and attempt to cut them off. I gunned the engines, turning hard to port and sped off leaving white froth in my wake as the Raider lifted and careened over the water. We were making good progress when we received a second message from the Hong Kong Police Patrol Boat. They were chasing the contact, a very fast speedboat and were asking for us to also intercept the craft that was steering in our direction.

Our boat was no more than half a mile away and we pushed every ounce of speed from our craft as we bobbed and jerked over the waves of the sea. Suddenly, I saw a flare shoot up in the distance and go high into the sky like a firework, it then popped, casting a huge bright light over the sea area. Momentarily Lau and I stunned to see its red glow hanging carelessly in the sky, until I caught sight of the speedboat racing over the sea with its white mist being thrown up behind it. We closed the distance between the two craft down to no more than 200m and suddenly, without warning the speedboat changed course to starboard. I threw the boat into a hard turn and managed to claw our way up alongside the speedboat. By now we were no more than 20–30ft away from each other and I could make out the silhouettes of people inside the craft in a frenzy of activity. Suddenly the speedboat changed course again and turned hard left. Before there was any time to manoeuvre out of the way, the two boats collided and for a few fleeting moments the speedboat rose out of the water and on to the top of ours before falling back into the water. The collision sent Lau backwards onto his arse and I was knocked hard off my feet into the side with an almighty bang.

Bastards! I thought as I felt the wind knocked out of me, as if all the air had been dispelled.

We continued to hold course though; I was in agony by this stage and not realising the damage I'd done to my back. We began to circle the speedboat which by now had stopped and I saw passengers pointing in the water. Lau was back on his feet and excitedly calling to me. I slowed the engines to hear him over the din, he shouted that there were "people in the water" and I looked over the side to sure enough see a number of heads bobbing in the dark, murky waters. There were people frantically clinging to wood trying to stay afloat, and in that moment, I saw Lau point towards two heads close by. Directing me to them, he dragged in the first male and then another, only they turned out to be young kids wet, shaken but none the worse for wear. Meanwhile I had squeezed the handset on the radio and called in a message to all other craft warning them of our location and of the people in the water.

We fished out as many as we could and by now the police craft was alongside us helping us taking control of the situation as well as detain the three culprits who were driving and crewing the speedboat. It later turned out at their prosecution, that some 24 youngsters were onboard the speedboat being smuggled into HK and, upon seeing the police craft, had made a break for it. After the speedboat had collided with us, several of the kids had gone overboard into the sea. Whether this had been deliberate or accidental we never found out. We had stayed and searched for over an hour for the missing children but had only managed to pick up three out of the water with no sign of the others. Police later announced the missing children had drowned after their bodies were found. It had been a sad day and a senseless loss of life, which had left me in a sad state of how people were willing to risk everything for a little money and a chance of a new life.

The case went to court and the three smugglers were tried and sentenced for transporting illegal immigrants as well as manslaughter. The death of an adult is hard, but the death of kids is harder to bear, for anyone.

Tony's personal security tip: *Don't leave messages for your delivery men, it invites burglars who will know you're away.*

MEMORIES OF IRAQ 03:

(2007) one of the many typical types of security escort duties. Convoys could extend upwards of 10–20 cargo trucks with as little as 4–6 gun teams dependant on their requirement and destination. Teams had to avoid all manner of high risks or threats including: deadly hidden explosive devices, ambush positions, car bombs, riots/protests, allied military convoys, suicide bombers, Iraqi army operations and general civilian traffic. Teams also had to deal with vehicle breakdowns, tyre changes, medical emergencies, refuelling issues, negotiating irate police checkpoints, corruption/extortion and a whole host of other hidden dangers all on their own. © R. Stevenson

MEMORIES OF IRAQ 03:

(2005) 'Bomber' our resident camp mascot, as he takes a cool dip in the waters of the River Tigris, near Kirkuk. Dogs and European expats flocked together with big hard scary men going goo-goo over these adorable creatures. However, Iraqis were not always keen on dogs and were incredibly cruel. By the time we left Iraq, a number of animal charities were formed to help them. © R. Stevenson

Gurkha Chicken Cutlets

This recipe will make about 8 good-sized portions.

Gurkhas are amazing cooks and their food is often full of flavour, heat and enjoyment when tucking in. This special dish packs a punch that will stave off any hunger pangs.

INGREDIENTS:
1x deboned chicken pieces
1x dollop of olive oil
2x finely chopped onions
2x cloves of garlic, finely chopped
1x tablespoon of ginger
1x teaspoon of curry powder
1x teaspoon of cinnamon powder
1x teaspoon of turmeric
3x green chillies finely chopped

COATING:
1x whisked egg yolk & white
4–5 slices of white bread (crusts removed and blended finely)

METHOD:

Using plastic wrap, place the deboned chicken pieces individually into plastic wrap and pound (or roll them) into flat even pieces. This is to allow for even cooking.

Whisk 4 eggs in a single bowl and add a dollop of milk and season with the ginger, cinnamon, curry powder, turmeric, salt and pepper. Now blend the de-crusted bread slices to a fine consistency and place into a separate bowl. If desired you can add some grated cheese to the bread mix if you feel adventurous.

On a medium heat, preheat a large frying pan with the oil and cook off the onions, garlic until the onions begin to turn opaque.

Meanwhile, taking the individual chicken pieces from the plastic wrap, dip the pieces first in the egg-yolk mix and then liberally cover them in the bread mix so that they are fully coated in both mixes.

REMEMBER to always wash your hands and wipe the surfaces after handling raw chicken

Turn the heat up to a moderate heat and place the covered chicken pieces into the frying pan, cooking gently for about 25–30 minutes. Occasionally turn the chicken pieces over with a wooden spoon until the chicken has cooked through and the outer layer is a nice golden brown. **Do not allow ingredients to stick or burn.**

Once cooked place them on a plate and allow to rest for 1–2 minutes and drain of oil. Serve with boiled rice and/or chopped salad.

And a large ice-cold glass of Tiger Beer.

The Gentle Assassin

SUREN

- *Former:* Singapore Police Force Gurkha Contingent.
- *Active Service:* Singapore.
- *Security:* Sixteen years private security in Iraq, Afghanistan, South Africa, South America.
- *Additional:* Connoisseur of fine single malt whiskeys.

(2003–4) Oil fires burning in the Al-Rumalyah oil fields. Saddam Hussein ordered all the refineries and drill heads destroyed prior to the invasion of allied forces in 2003. It took years of work to put the fires out and the machinery working again. © R. Stevenson

It was the beginning of cold winter in Iraq, which none of us men of Nepal or India expected. I must say that I had never experienced any weather of this kind before, as I am from India and a place called Darjeeling, famous for its tea plantations and warm climates. For more than half of my life I had lived and worked in Singapore on an army exchange programme with a Gurkha police contingent under a British Force. Now though, I had completed my service and had moved into the world of private security and into the dangerous arena that was Iraq.

We were travelling-working-operating in the Northern Iraqi city of Kirkuk alongside the US Military in the large airbase on the outskirts of the city. From here we lived, ate, slept and operated as we moved our clients from any one of our various projects around the countryside. We were a small band of security men, just eight Gurkhas and six British expats and over that time we got to know each other very well.

The location and our work were not without hassle, there was a risk every day, even just living on the base as we were regularly alerted to *'incoming'* alarms as mortars and rockets exploded in and around the base. It was a big challenge of survival, but the days passed in a mix of risk and fun, harmony and balance in this crazy, high-risk theatre. When we were not operating, we conducted training periods, practising our weapons handling, anti-ambush drills, debus drills, cross-decking drills, escape procedures and vehicle maintenance periods. Sometimes it was lots of fun to have the same exercise, which we had also been though during our army careers and now we were doing the same once more to keep ourselves fit and strong and, of course, most importantly, to keep us alive.

Towards the end of the year, for our culture it was now the season of festival. We were heading towards one such festival called *Dashera/Dashain* which celebrates the victory of good over evil. At home there would be 14–15 days of celebrating this most important festival of the year, but for all of us former Gurkhas in Iraq, we were far away from our families and friends. Even so, we still planned to celebrate together. We asked for and got permission from our clients, and our leaders, to have a few days off to celebrate the event, and we began to make our plans. Firstly, we informed our manager that we wanted to celebrate our festival and we needed a sacrifice. Looking pleased that he wasn't the one we wanted to sacrifice, we agreed that we would bring in a local goat in order to pray to our God Durga and make the offering.

It was important to use our most famous of knives, the Gurkhas' *'Kukuri'"* for the ceremony, this was very important and our chosen former Gurkha who would perform the service spent the day sharpening his Kukuri to a fine, sharp blade. This would protect us from any kind of evil power. On the day of our Dashera celebration we sacrificed the goat and spent the remainder of the day cooking the fresh meat for the evening meal and the start of the festival. We invited our international expats and members of our client team to the meal and at the allotted time we began.

The evening was quite crowded with our friends and colleagues with all of us enjoying the time-honoured tradition with some drinks and goat curry. In cooking the meat, we had used a traditional Gurkha-style recipe that made the meat tender, as well as very hot and spicy. It was also our tradition to not waste any part of the animal, so we cooked everything that was edible, meat, intestines, heart, liver, some of its blood and even the goat's testicles.

The drinks and curry were served to everyone and everyone was enjoying the food, all loving the home-made meat curry. Suddenly one of our expats said he had eaten one of the *'egg kind of things'*, which was very tasty asking, "What was that?" All the Gurkhas heard him and broke out into fits of laughter. They shouted back at Robbie that he had eaten the main meat of the night, which was the testicles of the goat! All of us were laughing hysterically, even the other expats. Suddenly Robbie stood up and ran out the room and started vomiting. It was the bad experience for him.

After 14 months of working in Kirkuk, we were all relocated to Basra in southern Iraq for another project. This was where I first met my mate, Alan Boyd, who was one of the new expats who'd come to work with us. He was my team leader, very gentle and a badass. Of all of the expats I had worked with, Alan was the first British expat who became a very good friend of mine and we often worked together. By now I had been promoted to one of four project, senior Gurkha leaders.

We (Alan and I) worked very closely together, often fixing issues in the team, problem-solving on missions or sorting out general problems that come from multi-cultures working together.

Iraq's southern desert is probably one of the best shooting ranges I have ever been on. There are lots of burnt-out old tank hulks to shoot at so there should be no excuse for not having a perfect zero on your weapon. One morning Alan's phone rang. It was Mrs Boyd.

"Honey, do you need your car insurance to get your MOT?" she asked before adding, "or do the insurance people need to see your MOT first and do you need your old tax disc before they will give you a new one at the post office…? And what's all that shooting I can hear?"

Alan replied, "It's OK honey, we are just having a practice shoot with the lads and anyway I have Suren here looking after me so please don't worry."

"Let me speak to him please," came the reply

Mrs Boyd then had me agreeing to all her demands and instructions. In short, I had just been made Alan's personal bodyguard and had sworn a loyal oath to protect him and make sure he came home safe. Now here lies the problem, if you have ever worked with Gurkhas before you need to know one thing: 'they do exactly what it says on the tin'. There are no grey areas with Gurkhas, and I had sworn an oath to Alan's wife to protect him and this was now personal, a matter of faith and honour.

As a PSD Team leader you can sometimes have quite a few things all going on all at once: a radio in your ear, the vehicle radio blurting out verbal traffic, a satellite phone, a mobile phone and a client asking questions and making demands. Usually this all happens as you are trying to navigate your way through the city or avoiding any of the out-of-bounds areas, or dodgy police checkpoints and that's all before anything actually happens.

I made it my mission though, to make sure that every time Alan stopped, moved, transited or looked my way, I would have his back covered, with the butt of my weapon in my shoulder, looking over my sights and covering my arcs. Further to that, I made sure the team operated as one fluid unit taking some of the pressure off Alan. He had enough to worry about without worrying about the smaller stuff.

With new powers in Iraq and a corrupt arrogant attitude that screamed "I'm going to mess you around, just because I can," we entered one of the many checkpoints one morning on our way into the city. As soon as the vehicle stopped, another Gurkha and I stepped out and watched our north and south of our positions looking for any possible signs of danger. As Alan got out to speak to the police officer, who looked bored or lazy or both, I was standing to Alan's left.

Alan asked the guard who he worked for and the guards reply was, "Oil Police, I want $100 for you to pass through the checkpoint." These were notoriously corrupt officials in Basra and not even a real police force, just thugs in uniform protecting the oil fields of Iraq *(allegedly)*. They were constantly looking for any reason to take money off passers-by and we security teams were prime targets of their corruption games. Many a team had fallen foul of them or were unnecessarily held up if they refused to play their games.

Alan said, "No, not police. Ali Baba, you ask for $100, you are not police!" (NB: 'Ali Baba' was a widely used term meaning thief, as in Ali Baba and the Forty Thieves). At this, he pushed Alan hard in the chest catching him off balance, with the weight of his body armour making him take a step backwards and just managing to stay on his feet.

In one single movement, I pulled my shining *Kukri* knife from under my left arm with the speed of a guillotine and brought the flashing curved blade down in front of the guard's face stopping mere inches from his nose. I then pulled the knife back, through the air holding it high above his head and paused: the next swing would cut the guard's head in two like a soft watermelon.

I screamed at the man, "You do not touch, you do not touch!"

I watched as all the blood drained from the guard's face as he realised how close he had just come to being decapitated.

Slowly I lowered my razor-sharp blade and re-sheathed it, in a way that had everyone see the beauty and the horror of the thing. I held onto the handle of my *Kukri* ready and primed for anything and the guard—just like every bully in the world, paused, realising that the severity of this situation was now out of his control and he crumbled and stepped back. His bluff had been called, the corruptive sham was over and we could now get on with the day's work with one less bribing official to deal with. Sadly, corruption was everywhere and this was typical of what we had to go through regularly.

In the end, our project end came in sight. As the project drew down to its conclusion, my team became the only team left for those final few days, with me as the supervisor, Alan my Team Leader and Robbie my Operations' Manager. I had time to reflect on the five years I had spent working alongside my former Gurkhas and expats, many of whom I now considered my friends. I very much enjoyed working with Alan and we had lots of good times and bad times together. I was pleased that we had stayed together until the project closed, right to the end, where we would finally turn the lights out and lock the doors behind us.

In that July, I left Iraq and went home to Darjeeling. Alan and Robbie moved on to other projects and over time we just lost touch. In 2016, by good fortune, I found myself once more back in Iraq, Baghdad to be precise, and I met up with Robbie once again. We spent all night talking through all the old times we had been through together and everything that had occurred since we had seen each other, it was great to meet up with old friends again. I was saddened to hear about Alan's passing from leukaemia; this was the first time I had heard the news and it hit me hard. That night we both shed tears for our special friend and I said a silent prayer for my long lost and dear friend.

In our lifetime we make lots of friends and some come and some go, but there are some people who leave us with good memories such that we can't forget them even if we try to. Alan Boyd was that kind of person and I will never forget him; he was such a generous person, a friend, a brother that will always remain in my heart.

Suren's Personal Security Tip*: Never eat yellow snow…*

Convoy Crew Beef Stew

Another tasty meal cooked as a team meal where they can get stuck in and share over the same pot. Time must be given to allow the mix to cook through thoroughly but is well worth the wait. This meal serves 4 and is easy to prep.

INGREDIENTS:
1x large pack of beef (approx. 15 oz)
2x tins of chopped tomatoes
1x medium potato per person (chunky chopped)
1x chopped onion (chunky chopped)
1x carrot per person (chunky chopped)
1x mug of frozen peas

1x teaspoon of black pepper
1x tablespoon of corn starch
1x pint of beef stock
3-4 mugs of water

METHOD:

Preheat the oven to 200°

Peel and chop the potatoes, carrots and onions and place in a large cooking pot. Then roughly chop the beef into 2cm cubes and add them to the same pot. Add both tins of tomatoes and add the pepper along with the beef stock. Place the pot in the oven and slow cook for 2 hours stirring occasionally.

Meanwhile, in a small bowl, mix the corn starch and water until you achieve a smooth consistency and add/stir into beef mixture after 1 hour. Return to the oven and continue to cook stirring periodically.

After two hours, check the mix and either continue to cook further or remove and rest depending on your own preference.

Ladle the mix into four medium-size bowls and serve with fresh warm bread.

A delighted team will be amazed at how simple this creation is and it will definitely go some way to cementing your place as a decent cook in the team.

It's a Mine, It's a Yours

GARY

- *Former*: SNCO 2nd Battalion the Parachute Regiment.
- *Active Service*: Northern Ireland, Belize, Afghanistan, Iraq.
- *Security*: Southern Iraq.
- *Additional:* Tier-2 Medic.

(2005) A former Gurkha security guard watches over the desert camp from the only high point in the desert, the perimeter sand berm. © R. Stevenson

It had been a typical day in southern Iraq and not much was happening. There had been no major incidents for a while now although the high threat continually hung in the air with a sense of menace. Our mission this particular day had been one of a QRF — *Quick Reaction Force* for the project, covering both north and south of the Al-Rumalyah oil fields and overwatch for some twenty-five teams who were out and about. Today, it had been both Alan and I running the QRF team, which consisted of two expats and four former Gurkhas, our security men.

It was drawing towards the end of the working day, but there was still plenty of light left before all the teams would call it a day; they would then collapse from their positions and begin returning to base. As the QRF, it was our responsibility to be the last team in. Suddenly a call came in from our Operations Room.

In the exchange that followed, details came over the mobile phone that one of our sister teams had been caught up in an unmarked minefield. One of their vehicles had become disabled after hitting an anti-personnel mine and we had heard that at least one person was injured. We were tasked to

(1): move to the area

(2): report in what we found

(3): assist where we could.

With the details plotted on the map and the team informed of what was happening, we moved off from our position.

After only a short drive we managed to arrive at the scene. The metalled road we were on was a straight north-south road, but off to the west, some 150m in a large expanse of rolling dried grass, we saw our two stationary security vehicles. We quickly located a nearby Bedouin track just to the north of our position and when we followed this it brought us close to where the team were positioned by some 50 metres as near as dammit.

We quickly established that both of their two security vehicles were stuck in the field with the lead vehicle immobile after it had run over an unmarked anti-personnel mine. There was damage to the front axle of the vehicle and we could clearly see this vehicle wasn't going anywhere. What we didn't know at the time was that they had also run over an anti-tank mine which had failed to detonate, this only came out later during the debrief. The second, or rear vehicle, was still mobile but hadn't moved from its position when it had come to a stop. From our position, we were now close enough to call out to each other. All of their personnel were OK, but the engineer had caught some small fragments in his wrist and hand during the blast.

As we were making an assessment of the situation, a second QRF team arrived on the scene but remained on the north-south road. They provided cover from the road while Alan and I decided on our next move. To our west, I noted that there was a Bedouin camp, further away from the incident and by now the local Bedouin, although at a distance, were starting to gather. They were no threat to us, merely curious so we paid them little mind.

There was little time left in determining why/how the team had driven into the minefield and with late afternoon wearing on, time was now a major factor and we needed to establish a way of getting the team out safely and quickly. From our location, we were over an hour away from our main home base and even if we called in for military support, by the time the message was relayed, the military then mobilised and their travel time to our location, it would have been very late in the day. *And* the military did not operate at night… or in a minefield, come to that.

The second QRF had a client EOD Engineer (explosive ordinance disposal) with them who by now had established communications with the trapped team's engineer. But very little in the way of solutions were coming from either the second team, or their first engineer. Time was wearing on.

Reluctantly, the second engineer volunteered to sit on the hood of our vehicle and guide us in along the route taken by the trapped team. They had already proven this route when they had driven in and as nothing else had detonated, we deemed it a safe enough plan to use. It was risky, but it was all we had to go on in that moment.

The plan was to slowly drive in along the tracks of the first team, guided by the engineer on the bonnet and using the same tyre lines as the trapped team. We would then collect the crew and back out again. When the plan was pitched, the second security team were not only not very keen on the idea but also voiced their objections. So Alan looked at me and said, "Gaz, are you game?" I said, "Fuck it, we have to get them out sooner or later."

We then chatted with the second engineer who was now under extreme pressure to get moving. However, neither Al nor I were impressed by his attitude that seemed a little dogmatic and unwavering as he briefed us. When it came to tracking in, I briefed the engineer with a simple set of instructions, I told him to, "sit on the bonnet and just point in the direction you want me to travel". As soon as we set off, he started acting like a twat, banging on the bonnet and arrogantly jabbing the air in the direction he wanted us to go.

After a while this became irritating and Al said, "I wish we could sort him out," so without hesitation, I slammed on the brakes. The next few seconds were a picture! As I hit the brakes, the engineer started clawing at the bonnet frantically trying to stay on the vehicle; his eyes were as wide as a bulldog's bollocks and on his face was an expression of just sheer fucking terror. When he finally composed himself back on the bonnet, I gave him the thumbs-up and told Alan, "I think he got the message." Alan burst out laughing.

We eventually got to the trapped team, having driven carefully and slowly following their previous course. With time and daylight quickly running out, we managed to cross-deck all the lads into our vehicle before driving back out the same path we took in. We also managed to guide back the second trapped security vehicle onto the Bedouin track. The first engineer, who had minor injuries, was quickly patched up and transferred to the second QRF team. It was a relief for all of us and we had managed to do it without any loss of life and without further incident.

Disappointingly, when we reached the north-south road, the second QRF team started whingeing that we "shouldn't have done that," that "they [the trapped team] should have stayed where they were until the military turned up." What they were verbalising was that, neither one of them had the bollocks to do the job themselves.

The second team departed with a very forlorn engineer, along with the second EOD vehicle and the rest of the trapped team. We, in the meantime, remained on the hard standing waiting to find out what was to happen to the damaged EOD vehicle that was still in the minefield. Robbie, our operations manager, cleared us to destroy the vehicle in place and we notified the Bedouin of our intentions, ensuring they remained at a safe distance before we then planned our next move.

As neither of us wanted to go back into the mine field, we had the idea that both Alan and I would fire our weapons simultaneously at the fuel tank using some of the tracer rounds we carried in our magazines, this would hopefully set the vehicle on fire. However, in reality, this only happens in films and not in Iraq. After some 200 rounds and switching from our AK-47s to the team's machine gun, a Russian-made RPK, on fully automatic, we did eventually get the vehicle alight, but only after some of the rounds had set fire to the vehicle's flammable interior. Once we ensured that the vehicle was fully engulfed in flames, we mounted up and set off back to base and reported on the event.

Back at base, we gave the details of the incident over to Robbie and closed down for the night. It had been a good day and we had managed to pull out the trapped team and get everyone home safely, can't say fairer than that, can you?

Gaz's personal cookery tip: As Para Reg, when we cook anything in the field two spoons of curry powder sorts everything out.

Hobo Meals

The Iraqi way to barbecue your food if you fancy getting together over a couple of cold ones at the end of the day.

Serves up to 8 persons

INGREDIENTS:
1 lb meat cut into cubes. Approx. 2cm
Locally grown vegetables — peeled and cut into small cubes. Approx. 2cm
1x full clove of garlic
1x Tblsp butter per wrap
1x sprinkling of mixed spices per preference: chilli powder, curry powder, meat spices

Tabasco hot sauce
Tinfoil

METHOD:

Using a BBQ Grill, (makeshift or otherwise) heat up the wood/coal fuel and allow time to reach its normal heating point.

Peel, cut and dice the vegetables of your choice into 2cm squares. Wash and cut the meat into similar size squares. Now taking a piece of tinfoil approximately 6x 6 inches, place a handful of meat and vegetables into the middle of the tinfoil and add spices (your own personal preference), 1–2 cloves of garlic, tablespoon of butter, splash of Tabasco sauce and wrap the foil up tightly not allowing for any of the contents or butter to seep out.

Place on the BBQ for at least 40 minutes — or longer dependant on how well done you like your meat. Remove from the heat and place to one side to rest for 1–2 minutes and then eat.

The New Beginning

TOM

- *Former:* Corporal, Royal Artillery.
- *Active Service:* Belize, Germany, Kenya, Northern Ireland.
- *Security:* Fifteen years' security service in Iraq, Afghanistan.

Camp Appleby in the West Qurna oil field. The camp was in the middle of nowhere, giving an Alamo feel to the place. It was surrounded by miles of flat, open countryside and hundreds of different tribes, all with their own unique issues and challenges. © R. Stevenson

The captain had announced that we were starting our descent and had lowered the landing gear. Reality came rushing back to me and my work mind started sinking in, as we were headed to Basra International Airport, as it was called. In real terms, this was just a small hub of an airport where the Iraqi immigration police, or whatever uniform they decided to wear that day (or their mood come to that), were the deciding factor on what items they could take off you and which would most likely end up being sold down the local market at the best price. What they would try to confiscate from unsuspecting passengers, was a game of cat-and-mouse and it really came down to whether you could outwit them that day. It was a game, sometimes you won and sometimes you didn't.

Every expat flying into Basra knew there was a high chance they were going to lose some items from their luggage, it was just a matter of keeping your good kit and equipment hidden as best you could and letting them think they had got something over you when the official confiscated items. And, all the while this was done with a nicotine-stained toothy smile, like the keys on a piano and the overuse of poor-quality hair dye left them looking slightly ridiculous. This always amused me especially in the Iraqi men of this generation I met; I would hardly ever see an Iraqi man without his hair or facial hair unkempt. Even the older men frequently dyed their hair, hanging on to the last remnants of their youth, trying never to see a morsel of grey showing through.

Today was my lucky day though. As I walked up to the immigration counter, I could see in the background an Iraqi official smiling and waving. I didn't think for one moment that it was directed at me, but as I got closer the gentleman stepped up to the counter and said, "You don't recognise me, do you?"

I suddenly had that awkward moment where I was trying hard to recollect who he was or wondering whether this was just a simple case of misidentification. Then from the fathoms of my mind, the penny dropped and I found myself remembering a face I hadn't seen in many years.

Three years prior, I had two Iraqi brothers working in my security team. Sadly, one of the brothers had been killed during some local inter-tribal fighting, or so I had been told. This had been at a time when both the military and contractors had first entered Iraq. During this period, the only form of real employment opportunities for Iraqis was to work directly for an international subcontractor organisation or the allied military. This was very dangerous especially for local men, as the militias, who were just local gangs of thugs influenced and supported by Iran, would regularly seek out and kill any local personnel they found working for, or helping, the foreign militaries and international contractors.

His name suddenly came to me. "Ahmed!"

He looked at me, surprised that I even remembered and for the next few minutes we talked and recollected the years we had worked together and the time that had passed since last we saw each other. There was still a bond a friendship there that I wished a higher percentage of Iraqis would have, but as you travelled through some of the towns and villages you could see the utter contempt and hatred some of them had for us. It was as if, every one of 'us' was to blame for the country's troubles. We spoke at length and sadly his brother had become another statistic for the militias, after they killed him for working for the US government agencies, and not after tribal fighting as I had been led to believe. Ahmed, after burying his brother, had left the security world and moved into the newly formed Iraqi Security Forces. With promises of staying in touch, we exchanged numbers and I made my way through the rest of Arrivals and out into the main terminal area.

As I entered the expansive hall of the airport, I noted it was packed with people. There were some fifty or so 'local fixers' all with signs for various companies, mainly oil and gas companies who were operating in the south. This rush of International Oil Companies (IOCs) into Iraq, post fighting now over, were our new clients and quickly changing the entire way of thinking in the south. With the organisations came new rules, concepts and regulations, pushing the boundaries on security safety to the outer limits and one that all of us would need to adapt to quickly if we were to contractually stay active in Iraq.

Just then, I saw in the corner of my eye, a flash of my company sign, and a bored, tired and listless local fixer resting the sign lazily on his lap. He was about as interested in this task as he would be in quantum physics and I sighed deeply, looking around me at the flurry of influential local personnel or good fixers, all of whom had been snapped up by the oil and gas companies. These lads were on a pretty penny with the oil companies, whereas the ones who worked for the security companies were on about a quarter of the wages. So I understood why he really had no get up and go; to be honest, who would want to sit around an airport all day with broken toilets and no shops selling decent cups of coffee/tea? It was a thankless job but even so… I sighed again.

After the tired and well-used welcome and ice-breaker conversation, the fixer took out his phone from his pocket and made a call to the waiting team. Once outside, two familiar faces greeted me and we shook hands like long-lost friends. Alan and Scotty were the company ad-hoc team; in fact, there were three of them in the team with Robbie, the third operator, currently away on R&R. I nicknamed them all 'the Three Amigos' as they had worked together for years and were virtually inseparable. I had worked with Scotty on previous contracts and had met Alan and Robbie sometime later when they had travelled to our Headquarters in Baghdad. Both Alan and Robbie were former 'Royals' (Royal Marines) and as always, upon meeting them, you would get the customary "Hello shipmate," as Marines tended to do. Scotty, like me, had been army so at least we spoke the same language. Thank God!

Eventually we reached the billet for my overnight stay situated in the top end of the airport and I crashed for the night, sleeping the sleep of the dead. I woke the next day to find out that I was going on to a new contract start-up project. We were to travel some two and half hours north of Basra and up into the middle of a volatile tribal area, a location where they talked matters through with AK-47s. I had also been briefed that Alan would be coming up a week later to train up the new local team and who would work alongside me. It was a one-year contract guaranteeing me work for that period, but one that would test me to my limits as a security professional and manager.

The journey up was without incident and when we arrived at my new home for the next eight weeks, my heart sank. Reality kicked in as soon as we entered the camp, known to all of us as 'Camp Appleby'. I looked around this tiny, dilapidated location, no more than 100 ft across in any two directions and which had hastily been thrown together using fly-by-night local contractors just the week before. It was so rundown I thought I'd come to the wrong camp at first. The watchtower sangers were made of wood and had no protection from weather nor would they stop a pea-shooter, let alone live ammunition. The accommodation was an old, rusted shipping container literally covered in inches of dust and dirt. There was trash everywhere: oil spills over the pebbled courtyard, no working toilets and sandbags were only half- filled or, spilling their contents out onto the dry, dusty ground. In truth, it was more like a large kitty litter box than a camp.

Further issues struck me as I spoke with my new team supervisor. He only spoke the smallest amount of

English; in fact, barely any English at all and the guard were nothing short of a ragtag, scraped together crew from various local tribes, possibly all the dross and village numpties that could be gathered together. With the barest of basic security training and not an English word between them, I sighed deeply again and thought, *Bloody hell! I've a lot of work ahead of me,* and Alan could not arrive soon enough.

When he finally arrived, I was ecstatic; at least I had extended help and my worries were halved by having another expat with me. Right from the get-go, Alan and I got to work like demons. Firstly, we loaded up over a thousand sand bags and placed them around our camp defences, the sangers, the gates and anywhere else they were much-needed. At least the guards would have some form of protection. We beefed up the access/egress gates, outer defences and installed barbed wire around the outer perimeter and top of the camp. We got the guard to help clean the camp from top to bottom of all its rubbish and swept the containers clean, disinfecting them, ready to install the furniture that was in-bound later that week.

Later that day, we hired a local chef who had spent at least ten years in Europe and had decide to return to Iraq to put to good use the culinary skills he'd learnt abroad. Officially, he didn't start work for another five days and so he got stuck into the kitchen to start preparations and get supplies organised. A few days later, the chef managed to get hold of some fresh rations and Alan and I were glad to stop living off our issued MREs (the US version of British army rations). This meant that night, Alan and I cooked a much-needed hot, fresh meal for ourselves. The only trouble was that Al's culinary skills were much better than mine so, I leant on him further with cooking for the two of us. My cooking skills were shocking; I would burn salad, so I was reliant on Alan to cook tasty things, fresh things, edible things and that left me to worry about the camp and its inhabitants. It seemed to work well and Alan seemed at home in the kitchen.

Days settled into a routine and to say that we felt a little like Rorke's Drift would be an understatement. We were virtually alone and miles from anywhere. We became reliant on ourselves and all the knowledge we had in soldiery in setting up defences; we looked for weaknesses and did our best to plug the gaps. At least at Rorke's Drift they had a hundred men highly trained and ready to fight if needed. What we had were the flotsam and jetsam of tribes: the unemployable, the young and the restless; the bored, fat and uninterested. It was an uphill challenge, but never ones to back down from a fight, Alan and I spent day after day, week after week doing our best to instil some security knowledge and training into the guard so that we could at least have them up to a basic set of skills.

We worked them hard and trained and trained and trained. Some days it was a case of one step forward and two steps backwards, but we made slow progress. One of our biggest challenges was keeping them awake in the sentry sangars. It wasn't uncommon to wander around the perimeter at night and see the silhouette of a figure hunkered down wrapped in his blanket on the floor, gently snoring to the echoes of the night. It was maddening trying to keeping them awake and only made us more tired and frustrated. What we needed was to set an example.

Many weeks later, after continuous episodes of finding people asleep in sentry towers, we found the worst ten culprits—ones that had become what we call in military circles, 'untrainable'; people who, had they been trained or instructed for the next hundred years, would not move any further forward than where they were at the start. We let them go and told them to go back to their tribes and not to bother coming back. We had planned for this and already had the next ten tribesmen lined up to start work/training immediately and they slipped in easily enough but were only marginally better than those ones we released.

What we hadn't considered in our small triumph in ridding ourselves of ten problem children was the tribal politics involved. Unbeknown to us at that time was that each man of workable age paid a tithing to the tribal elder, a way of centrally supporting the tribe as such. Therefore, the more men they had working, the more money that elder had to control and support the village and the richer and more powerful that village became. So imagine his surprise when ten of his latest and newly employed men returned to the village and told him they had just been sacked for sleeping on the job. In his anger, he refused to accept this and tells them to return to the camp and get their jobs back and be pronto about it. So now imagine our surprise when we see ten newly dismissed men return to the camp gates demanding their old jobs back. They were then royally told where to go and that it was all too late for apologies, but further to this was they had now been replaced, so '*no*' you cannot have your jobs back.

So now imagine the village elder's surprise, thinking he had solved yet another one of the village's problems, when he spies his ten lads return to the village all forlorn and with their tails between their legs explaining that they cannot get their old jobs back. Worst of all they have now been replaced with a new set of guard from another village. In his fury, the village elder does not accept this and orders the men to go back and demand their jobs back and be double pronto about it and make themselves more forcefully heard or else… So imagine our surprise when we see ten recently dismissed employees return to the camp gates once again this time all armed to the teeth with AK-47s, pistols and laden down with many magazines, and all demanding their old jobs back… or else….

Inside the camp, we are now tested and I can see this is going south if things escalate. Blood begins to pump faster and breathing becomes heavier. Talks begin, but then start to breakdown as tensions and anger rise, there is now plenty of animated arm waving, loud shouting and threats of violence being made in Arabic. As things intensify, there is some jostling and pushing as the ringleader reaches new heights in his angered fervour. His finger-points and jabs at our security supervisor sent in to act as a liaison. He remains calm as our negotiating peacekeeper, but he is wavering, especially when a fat sweaty finger jabs him fully in the chest. How long will he maintain control? We know not. He is our herald and still the animation of flailing arms, shouting and finger-pointing goes on. Suddenly faces change, they scowl and purse; their body language takes a dramatic turn that announces that they — the group — have now passed a threshold of a peaceful solution. By now, the atmosphere becomes thick and heavy and you can feel it weave and ebb inside the camp like an enormous invisible, heavy cloud. We know we have reached boiling point; we cannot relent; it's gone too far now, and in any case, how can we ever trust those demanding men now?

Suddenly without warning there is a large audible metallic sound that echoes around the camp. A rifle has been cocked and distinct by the working parts pulled to the rear and released with the horrific sound of a round being chambered. This is quickly followed by another rifle cocked, followed by another and suddenly a dozen weapons are all cocked. From our side and across the camp, our security weapons are suddenly cocked and readied. Up in the sangar, a belt-fed PKC machine gun is readied and swings around towards the front gate at those threatening the camp. People are now backing away from each other, like gunslingers creating space inside the town before a showdown.

Meanwhile, I have grabbed by phone and called in our situation, passing all the details as they happen. Ops tell me a QRF is inbound, leaving in five minutes. It will take them just under two hours to arrive at our location and I start my calculations should the situation get worse. Alan has our clients bundled into safe rooms along with their grab bags; vehicles are loaded with spare ammunition; drivers switch on their ignitions and stand by ready to crash out of the camp taking our clients and us with them. Outside the camp the stand-off continues, like an old Western movie. One group sits and waits inside the fort while the second group spreads out and takes up positions among the sand berms in front of the camp, ready for the shooting to start. It will take just one match to light this powder keg and thank God we had trained our guards to a decent standard of weapon discipline.

Just then we are thrown a lifeline: the phone rings and its Ops telling me that they have managed to get hold of the local police force commander who is sending in two teams of police to deal with the situation. They arrive some forty minutes later in two large grey/blue battered pickup trucks. A Captain who looks like the Iraqi equivalent of Tom Cruise — sporting aviator sunglasses no less — gets out and heads over to the tribal men. There is a conversation, followed by more shouting and then... at last... there is calm conversation. The discussion goes on some forty minutes and then it is all over and the tribesmen reluctantly go home. Whatever the topic of conversation was, whatever the promises that were made, or whatever the persuasion used to defuse the situation, I will never know. All I know is that a blood feud had just been avoided and I breathed out long and hard in relief. Later we find out the dismissed Iraqis will be re-employed elsewhere by the Russian oil company and just like that, the situation is over.

I stayed at the camp for the next year and oversaw a number of project changes and the project expand to new proportions, but the camp remained in its same state along with the constant need for attention and upkeep. And suddenly, like a giant wounded land whale, the project drew down and collapsed, as once again we lift and shift, heading south, back the welcoming bosom of Basra.

As we begin to pull out, the region only intensifies as tribal issues turn from frustration to jealousy to anger as numbers of different tribesmen are employed by the IOCs, which sees many tribes turn against each other with a series of bloody, violent events. They didn't mess around either; mortars, light and heavy machine guns, RPGs and grenades were all used as they attacked one another. Casualties are reported on all sides, a conflict that sees the police reluctant to interfere. And in that moment, I am only too glad when I get word that we are pulling out. It goes without a hitch and I am left to move onto another testing project in another testing part of the south... deep joy.

Tom's personal security tip: *If at first you don't succeed, try doing it the way your section commander told you to.*

MEMORIES OF IRAQ 04:

(2006) Range Day in Iraq. Consisted of using many weapons that were not conventional to UK forces. Weapons from various Chinese, Russian and Eastern bloc countries such as: AK-47s, Draganov sniper rifles, Tokarovs, RPKs, PKCs, PKMs SKS and a whole host of others. Even though we were no longer military, we maintained our key core skills, weapon ethics, discipline and practices to keep our skills honed. These much-needed skills and drills were often the difference between life or death on many occasions. © R. Stevenson

MEMORIES OF IRAQ 04:

THE THREE AMIGOS (2010) The last photo ever taken of all three of us together in Iraq, during a rare period of downtime at the American PX. A short time after this was taken, Alan returned home to Scotland. Within two years, Alan was diagnosed with Acute Myeloid Leukaemia and after fighting on so many foreign shores, his final battle would be on UK soil.

Fried Bread 'al-la Convoy'

When energy levels are dwindling and you need a pick-me-up, this dish is a great way to start firing on the cylinders once more and is a great way of giving the team a small boost at any time of the day.

INGREDIENTS:

2 slices sandwich bread
Mini sausage or equivalent chopped (like chorizo or salami from the PX)
1 egg (whisked) add pepper
1 teaspoon bouillon granules (OXO cube)
1 teaspoon soy sauce
1 tablespoon oil
50 grams Korean kimchi (from PX) or a sauerkraut if you cannot get it.
2 leaves lettuce (chopped)
Spring onions and tomatoes (chopped)

METHOD:

Chop up the bread into small cubes.
In a frying pan, heat some oil.
Add in all the ingredients and stir-fry for 2–3 minutes (add the whisked egg last to bind it all together).
Transfer to a plate and serve with chopped onions and tomatoes (with hot sauce is awesome!)

The Dirty Dogs of Al-Fatah

ANDY

- *Former:* SNCO, Scots Guards.
- *Active Service:* Belize, Germany, Northern Ireland.
- *Security:* Four years' security service in Iraq, including being the best operations manager you could ever want.

(2004) The Al-Fatah bridges, looking south. Tikrit is not quite visible but is top right of shot. During the 2003 campaign, the US mistakenly bombed the road bridge not knowing that several main supply oil pipes to the north lay underneath. The Al-Fatah camp was laid out just to the bottom right of shot. © R. Stevenson

We were called to a meeting late in the afternoon. For days now, a rumour had been circulating around the base that some poor wretches were being sent to northern Iraq to a project, known to most as *'Al-Fathah'*.

I had only been in country for a matter of weeks and since touching down in Baghdad, I had spent most of my time either escorting supply trucks back and forth along the infamous 'Route Tampa' or equally uninspiringly, stood guard expending endless hours in the baking heat of the Al-Rumalyah oilfields. This was my first gig on 'the circuit' and after having spent a couple of years out in Civvy Street, I had been drawn to Iraq by the potential of a little adventure and the fabled popstar wages. With 13 years' service in the Guards under my belt, I was less than impressed to discover that the Basra element of the security project was headed up by a couple of megalomaniac military underachievers who were clearly hell-bent on upsetting practically every fucker they came into contact with.

It was early summer of 2003 and my deployment had coincided with that of another five newbies. All but two had sensibly kept their heads down and their mouths shut, yet now in the meeting we clearly stood out as the fresh meat and fated to take the journey north. The meeting rattled off the names of those who were routinely designated to the following day's tasks before the serious topic of Al-Fatah was then raised. Of course, we all had heard rumours of how basic the living conditions were there and that the operating base itself, had unavoidably been located inside hostile territory, devoid of any real-time military support.

Geographically, it was surrounded by high ground, flanked by the Tigris River and with only the choice of two ways in and out, the site was considered an 'Alamo' in waiting.

As the meeting progressed, volunteers were called for, though in our present location the lure of washing machines and air conditioning with decent accommodation and food was too strong to defy. One by one, unsurprisingly, my fellow newbies were assigned to the northern pipeline project, but to my surprise I was not! Admittedly I felt a moment of relief as life around Basra, although incredibly mundane, was relatively safe compared to other areas of the country at that time. I spoke up, like some suppressed masochist suddenly getting the better of my reasoning. "I'll go," I said. "Look, clearly no one wants to go, so I'll take someone's place."

'That I meet in the Summer, Indian Summer...' The distant hypnotic piece by The Doors was interjected by the loud shrill of an aircraft alarm. I had nodded off listening to my iPod but was now awoken abruptly by an overexcited Mick, the inflight alarm blaring away and the terrified screams of an oversized roughneck sitting near me.

As I glanced beyond the seat in front of me and between the shoulders of the flight crew, I could see us dropping fast, heading almost vertically straight down towards the ground. I turned to face the former bootneck in the seat beside me.

"What the fuck's going on, Mick?" I asked while pulling my earphones out.

"Anti-surface to air drills," said Mick. "Apparently there's a threat in Kirkuk, so we need to descend rapidly."

With the fearful screams of our client still reverberating inside the tight confines of the fuselage, I sniggered wickedly back at Mick. "Scream if you wanna go faster!"

Once on the ground, the aircraft was met by our transport manned by a security detail of ex-Gurkhas and a couple of heavily bearded expats. We had now arrived in the oil-rich and ethnically divided city of Kirkuk, 148 miles north of Baghdad. A day later, I met Sammy, a fellow ex-G-man and over the following day, organised weapons and a trip to some makeshift US ranges. As an organisation, we favoured the accessible AK-47s and Browning Hi-Power pistols. Both systems had proven to be very reliable in our environment.

The following morning, driving south, it was quiet as we set off well before first light in order to get most of the way to Al-Fatah before daybreak. The road was mainly flat with the occasional settlement sporadically positioned en route. There was no stopping and we made good time until we reached the River Tigris, which was on the northern side of my new camp. The site had been a natural crossing point for many years, evident by two high, towering, but blown-out bridges once connecting the Governorate of Kirkuk to its southerly neighbour of Salahadin. The natural break in the mountains was wide, with river floodplains and vegetation on either side. The northern bank was much broader than the south, that saw a steady gradient up into what was now an equipment laydown yard that was the bulk of the clients' current workload and the mainstay of the project. The laydown yard was surrounded by a high dirt berm with periodic overwatch sentry positions. South, across the river, we could make out a small, fortified compound set back from the river, but in the shadow of the high ground to its south and western flank. There was a further work area outside the compound's walls, dominated by concrete towers, chicaned dirt tracks with manned checkpoints.

My brief from the project lead was simple: our clients' task was to bridge the gap with oil pipelines, specifically drilling them under the river and then to reconnect them to further oil lines which were under construction to the north. All we had to do was minimise delays and keep the clients alive—the latter of the two proving somewhat of a daily challenge due to our means of transport across the river.

As I settled in, security duties consisted of night and day shifts working 24/7. We were under constant threat of attack albeit after a few weeks, this heightened state of personal alertness did become the norm and so any sense of downtime inside the compound became invaluable to your own mental sanity. As rumoured, living conditions weren't fantastic, but they could have been a whole lot worse. The electricity was rationed, though water and food were of a good standard. Most of the security team were ex-infantry and so the fact that we had beds, three square meals and a spot of aircon in the evenings meant that we were happy enough. A few of us had access to laptops and so if you were so inclined, you could at times get some Skype time with the outside world. Life was simple: work, eat and sleep, except work was life and the daily extremes were entertainment.

As part of the security plan for the project, a sizeable local security team had been recruited, trained, and deployed on checkpoint and overwatch duties across the Al-Fathah site. The guard force had been brought together by a local Sheik. To show balance, a healthy mix of Kurds, Arabs and Turkmen employed with religious divides bridged by recruiting Sunni, Shi'a, Kurdish, Christian, Assyrian and a small number of lesser-known religions. Collectively they provided an invaluable outer screen of defensive activities, albeit the vast majority required constant supervision and mentorship. The expats had got to know many of these local security guards and while all but a few seemed dedicated to our efforts, there was an underlaying niggle that should attacks ramp up, many would simply melt away and possibly, in the worst case, join the attacking forces.

Since arriving, we had been periodically attacked by multiple 60/80mm mortars and 107mm rocket attacks which had been mounted against our compound and laydown yard. These occurred day and night, though none had been physically effective up to my arrival. However, the attacks were having a detrimental effect on our clients' mental health and their work effort. Understandably everyone was thinking that it was only a matter of time before the bad guys struck lucky and killed someone. On the returning transport, on the day I had first arrived, the convoy had gone back to Kirkuk with a couple of clients who were calling it a day due to the increased attacks.

A week or two into my tour and I had been working the night shift with Baz one evening, when Tony the project 2i/c had us pull straws to see who was to go on the following morning's fuel and supply run. This was the first occasion that a resupply had occurred since my arrival and so I was not familiar with protocol.

"So, a short straw means you're on the run?" I asked.

"No," explained Baz, "it means you're on the bomb, the guy who gets to drive the GMC pickup full of fuel cans."

With my first fuel run in mind, I listened intently over a brew, as a group of the blokes told me a story of a previous run and how one expat, Don, had earned his nickname, *'Moose'*. Don was quite a small fella so it seemed ironic he should be named after such a large beast. It turned out that the nickname was rather less to do with his physique and more so his appearance in the immediate seconds after an a large IED strike. The previous convoy consisting of three vehicles, two soft-skin Land Cruisers and a large 2.5 T truck, more commonly known as 'the Duce' had been hit by the IED whilst returning back to camp along the road outside the Baiji oil refinery and just a few miles out from our compound. Andy had been driving the Duce and Don was sitting high in the back of the truck as top cover. The third vehicle was driven by Robbie, with Ian riding shotgun next to him. The Duce had been laden full with fuel cans but was slow and cumbersome amidst the Iraqi traffic. The convoy looked clearly military making it a prime target for attack. As the convoy had dropped south past the oil refinery, it had been forced to push over to the central reservation after kids had run into the road deliberately. Moments later, the IED—consisting of two, bound-together 155mm shells, detonated between the fuel-laden truck and the rear Land Cruiser. Dirt and fragmentation from the blast blew upwards high and out from the road, enveloping the rear of the convoy in dust, dirt and thick black smoke. From where Robbie and Ian were sitting, it appeared that the Don seemed to take the lot! Although the convoy maintained momentum, driving on, Don appeared to have vaporised. The blast wave and concussion ripped through the rear vehicle slowing time and motion. Robbie was later to find that the blast had perforated his eardrum.

Don had taken to tucking his gloves into his helmetband and in that moment both men were overwhelmed by sheer relief to see Don peering from over the top of the armour plating at the back of the truck, his eyes as big as dinner plates and his gloves flapping in the wind looking like a magnificent moose. The luck of the Irish and a poorly executed ambush had saved Don's life and the legend of the Moose was born.

We made numerous replenishment runs during our time at the bridgehead, each one with its own saga to tell, but none more out and out crazy than the battle of Baiji, whereby our convoy survived a complex ambush mounted in broad daylight. This combined the enemy's use of RPG, small arms and sustained fire from one end of the town to the other. Had it not been for the level of skill of our operators, we wouldn't have emerged alive. We hadn't been carrying any clients that day thankfully and so back at camp later, we were able to unload weapons and get the kettle on. The noise of the ambush had been heard by those back in the compound and anyone close by had rushed to check on how we all were. Over time, we had all grown pretty close, the clients being a good set of fellas and while the vast majority were older than their security detail, the old-school experienced oilers had grown respectful of our efforts. It was a fair observation to make that most of the clients were in the latter stages of their careers and were, in many ways, like us. Just looking for a little adventure, or a story or two to tell in the bars back home and a little nest egg to help keep the real wolves from the door.

Our base was hostile and isolated; the water of the river was highly polluted with God only knows what and the mountains literally stank of sulphur. All of us had the shits at some point and aside from bombs and bullets there were also the bugs, snakes, and the monster bugs like the dreaded camel spider with its poisonous bite that would leave large gaping red sores on the unsuspecting skin of those bitten.

Eventually my leave period had come around and it was now my turn to get some well-deserved R&R. The convoy from Kirkuk was inbound and along with Tony and Mark, I took the final white-knuckle ride across the river in the rickety boat used to cross each day. Boat by definition, though, in reality it was a leaky crude Canadian canoe-shaped water rickshaw, piloted by a young Iraqi chap. He lived on the shore of the river within our operational footprint and each day provided a vital service ferrying us back and forth between project sites. Of course, lifejackets were provided, although had anyone actually gone overboard, the kit we carried and the strong current of the river pretty much guaranteed you were a goner.

Once I was back from leave in Kirkuk, Tony and I were catching up with the events of the past few weeks. Things had been relatively quiet for those left behind with just the usual rocket and mortar attacks. No fatalities or major damage as per usual, though all agreed the situation was becoming somewhat of a bore. We did however often have Apache and other aircraft fly overhead or circle our location for a while. In fact, the sheer presence of a couple of Apache flying in the skies above us scared the crap out of me, less the poor locals. It had long been decided to brief the local US military aviation units north and south of the river of our presence, location and project details with other vital information such as our dress codes and defensive positions. The last thing any of us wanted was to become another sad statistic of some over-pumped air ace's own Green Zone war story, just because we happen to carry AK-47s. At least we were equipped with some Infra-red Fire-Flies and reassurance that we wouldn't be 'zapped' by a passing night flight on the mountainside while checking on our local guard force positions.

The drive back down to Al-Fatah bridge baptised me in my first IED incident. As the sun was slowly rising on the horizon I had beside me Sanjay, a former Gurkha and driver who was busy sharing a volley of yawns as we approached the last 20km of our journey, which was just before the break in the mountains and our destination. I recollect watching what seemed like a distant figure shimmering through the heatwave across the desert plain to my right. Moments later the road directly to our front erupted! The tarmac road formed a fifteen-foot mushroom of stones, rocks and dust chased directly by the glass of our Land Cruiser windshield shattering inwards. The vehicle screeched and lurched to the right, as I pulled the wheel with my left hand. Sanjay hit the brakes and missed the crater by a mere few inches.

"Drive!" I shouted and Sanjay's reactions were milliseconds as we accelerated forward. Indra, our rear gunner in the back of the vehicle suddenly opened fire. I had made ready my weapon and was actively trying to identify what the Gurkha was shooting at. All I could see was desert scrub all around. The radio was alight with sitreps and the inside of the vehicle was fast filling up with hot smoking brass, some of which found its way down the back of my shirt.

"Stop firing!" I shouted. "What are you shooting at, Indra! What are you shooting at?"

The Gurkha stopped shooting, turned to me and with a vague look on his face said, "I don't know."

In that moment his statement seemed one the funniest things I'd heard and we all began to laugh. And that was that: yet another near miss; we proceeded forward with no casualties, onwards to the northern laydown yard, another fun-packed three months at Al-Fatah and an unforgettable memory of Sanjay shaking windshield glass from his hair like a model in a sun-drenched shampoo ad.

Eventually towards the end of the year, the project began to ramp down, the core of the clients' work having been completed and the second phase was to be handed over to another oil company and a different security contract. As we began preparing for our security handover, I took my last few glances around the area that had been my home for almost a year. We had survived countless mortar and rocket attacks, roadside IEDs and shootouts through a town, like some modern twist of an old Western movie. We had survived a persistent threat of being overrun by the local Iranian-backed militia. We had survived scorpions, spiders and snakes. All of which was incredible in itself, but for sheer horror nothing could top seeing the Tigris River fully ablaze, not once but twice, after militants had IED'd the oil pipes, sending kilometres and kilometres of flaming oil into the river. It had taken the oil company specialists several days to put out the blaze.

On the last day and with everything handed over to the new teams and clients, we withdrew and ended back in Kirkuk which would be home for the next two months before we left completely. It had been a life-changing experience and one I will never forget. Sadly, the camp later fell into disrepair after the situation in the north changed and the clients withdrew after it was felt that the situation there was untenable. Just a few years later it was to be the scene of some of the hardest fought-over regions in Iraq, after the extremist group ISIS captured the area and seized control. It would take the Iraqi forces a further two years to recapture it with large numbers of casualties on both sides. The area passed from one side to the other in a seemingly endless exchange of gun battles.

But for those of us who stood there before ISIS, it will always be Al-Fatah and the beginning of amazing change in the region for everyone. There are some days, here in the UK where I will smell burning refuse, or sweaty bodies or hear a piece of music familiar to me and I am transported right back there, back to the dust and heat and flies, but do you know what? I wouldn't change it for the world.

Andy's personal security quote: *The world is a barometer, responding to the pressures of those who serve security and those who would seek to abuse the need for it.*

Pan-Fried Mushrooms at Dawn

Without doubt a tasty morning treat prior to getting stuck into the day's chores. Quick, simple, and packed full of flavour, this dish got the team moving when empty bellies were growling.

INGREDIENTS:
1 x Armoured Personnel Carrier (optional)
4-5x medium-sized mushrooms, washed and sliced
1x tbsp of butter
2x slices of bread, or roll, or samoon (Iraqi-type pitta bread)
Salt and pepper to taste

METHOD:

Wash and slice the mushrooms thinly and place to one side. Preheat a pan and add in the butter and gently stir until the butter has melted and bubbles begin to form. Add the mushrooms and stir to allow the mushrooms to fully coat with the butter. Add a pinch of salt and pepper here or at the end to taste.

Prepare two slices of bread with butter as desired, or bread roll, or pitta bread as required. Once cooked, remove the mushrooms from the heat and drain them before liberally scattering across the bread. Season to taste and eat.

Additionally, brown/tomato sauce can be added to make a traditional type breakfast. Don't forget your mug of tea to accompany this dish.

To truly taste the experience, add a wide, open field (optional) on a summer's morning and drink in the surroundings whilst eating.

Contact

TIM

- *Former*: Royal New Zealand Armoured Corps, RNZAC, Queen Alexandra's Mounted Rifles.
- *Saw Active Service*: East Timor, Bosnia.
- *Security*: Fifteen years Iraq security, Operations Manager, Project Manager.
- *Additional*: As a project Operations Manager, he was busier than a Heathrow Aircraft Control Tower.

Early days after the Iraq invasion, US forces posted many signs denoting worldwide locations, many of which became standard convoy markers when travelling and used as reference points. © T. Goodman

We were a six-vehicle, gun-truck move which gave us a lot of firepower but, in addition we also had many of the slow-moving and cumbersome cargo trucks (14 + 2 Bobtails in total) to escort. This mission had been successfully completed over consecutive days, delivering fuck knows what to Sulaymaniyah (in the North) and we were in the process of heading back to Umm Qasr in the far south of Iraq. The trip up and drop-off of cargo went without a hitch and with no incident to report.

We were in the process of making our way south, heading towards Tikrit south of Sulaymaniyah, when Charlie, our Team Leader, called back that his gun truck was suffering a mechanical failure, which was beyond common, so he was now going to have to be towed by one of the spare Bobtails. A Bobtail or 'Bob' as they were more commonly called, is a truck cab with no trailer or cargo, that was used as a spare for emergencies. For control we'd placed a local security guard inside the Bob to keep the driver focused; it didn't always work but that was the plan. At FOB Speicher (Forward Operating Base), Charlie was hooked up to the Bob and we moved off again southbound along the infamous Route Tampa. While the cargo trucks were all empty, we had made good time for the next 100km. But now the convoy was moving a bit slower due to Charlie's vehicle being towed, but other than that it was normal running.

At the north end of the Balad Straits, we approached a large Iraqi Army (IA) checkpoint. It was deserted, which was a bad sign! We slowed the convoy right down, crawling at a snail's pace, as we chatted via the VHF to discuss our options. Inside the CP we couldn't see any bodies which would have been an indication they'd been attacked. Perhaps they'd just walked off and deserted their posts, which wasn't uncommon for such a poorly trained bunch of fuckwits. In the end we had a schedule to keep and little in the way of alternative route options, not without a huge loop around at least, so we decided to push through and make best speed to the far end of the straits.

On command, off we went, foot down on the accelerators and don't hold back. I was positioned in the second GT so had a good view of the road ahead. There were a further two GTs mid-convoy and then Charlie's GT (being towed by the Bob) and a final GT at the rear watching our backs. All in all, we were probably stretched out over 300 metres front to rear. We were flying by now, easily doing 100km/h, and although our truck drivers didn't hold radios themselves, they could sense something was wrong and they too weren't holding back. The first cargo truck was right up my arse and pushing me to go faster with the others in hot pursuit, which I couldn't do due to the broken GT being towed.

…And then all hell broke loose. As if a sudden mighty storm had suddenly erupted, rounds rained down on the convoy hitting both sides at once. They drummed away at the armour plating fitted to our trucks which is always a noise that I will remember fondly. It may sound fucked-up but, being shot at is one of the few things in my life that has truly made me feel completely alive. Blood rushed through my veins at a thousand miles an hour; my brain went into complete overdrive and I felt so alive, not coasting or cruising, not wondering where your life is heading, not hating those who were now against you. You feel enveloped, immersed in a brotherhood, knowing that those around you are just as scared shitless as you are and regardless of this fear, would stand beside you to the hilt, as you would for them (I loved this feeling). Being at the front of our convoy, my gun truck and cannon fodder Charlie took the initial weight of the attack and they were the first to get brassed-up. Within a heartbeat, our top gunners returned fire, taking aim at the flashes of rifle fire on both sides and squeezing off rounds trying to win this maelstrom of an attack. All of our trucks had satellite alarm systems installed. We all must have hit the red buttons at the same time, which would alert our HQ that we were in the poo (again). It would have been a sight, seeing all their large operational monitors start to bleat alarm tones and flash like a Christmas tree.

As rounds came down in a flurry, we tried to push through the ambush. About this time, we could all hear over the radio what can only be described as screaming (little girl screaming I will later recall), weird! There was no way we could stop to see what was happening so by sheer brute force we kept pushing, it's all we could do. Surely this ambush must have a limit. *If we can get through, then we could regroup,* I thought to myself... It didn't happen. Unbeknown to us then in that moment, it turned out that this ambush was well over a kilometre in length and we were only a few hundred metres inside the kill zone. The ambush had been well planned and well executed by the militants.

By now our entire convoy was enveloped, and it was fucked. From inside my truck, the noise sounded like I was inside a drum and ten arseholes were beating on the drum with bats, *hard*! As we sped forward, the gunfire only intensified, and I knew it was going to be a shitfight of the highest order. This was not to say that all the gunfire was coming one way. We were after all a 6xGT convoy team, with twelve pinion-mounted belt-fed 7.62mm Russian made PKCs on top of our trucks. Our top gunners did themselves proud with a fair bit of "fuck you" given back. They were firing, reloading, firing and reloading again like men whose lives depended on it. It was a glorious cacophony of noise that told me my life was indeed finite and if I didn't do my job then it was all over.

My family and their faces suddenly flashed through my mind, all the smiles and dreams, dates I had missed, unrealised hopes. All in the space of 2.36 seconds because I didn't have any sort of time to dawdle. So, up to now this had been a pretty heavy, but standard, sort of ambush. Lots of lead flying, lots of return fire, a bit of arse puckering for good measure, but otherwise our type of normal for convoys back in 2007. But now it took a turn for the worse.

The convoy was now starting to slow. We had taken so much damage that our vehicles were beginning to give out. Nearly all of the gun trucks and cargo trucks had lost tyres. The cargo trucks taking the brunt of most of the fighting, they were now resembling beaten up pieces of (sort of) rolling scrap… And then we were coming to a grinding stop, somewhere in the middle of the kill zone.

Bad, bad, bad, thinks I. What can you do?

We were in a precarious situation, a matter of literal life and death and so we did the only thing we could do. We did what the cowboys of old would have done when overwhelmed, we circled the wagons. OK we didn't make a perfect circle, but you get the idea. As I was at the front, mine and the second lead GT stopped; we came alongside each other and formed the front of two rows all the while our top gunners continued to shoot at anything they suspected of being an ambushing militant, and I got out.

Getting out of your gun truck in the middle of a contact is as bad as it gets in an ambush, because inside my wagon I am protected by two inches of nice cosy armour and bulletproof glass. Getting out meant I was in my Kevlar helmet and body armour which was all I had to protect me (and they were fucking rubbish). But someone had to direct the trucks and take control, so out I got. The truck drivers understood pretty quickly (from past experience) and formed two lines behind our trucks giving us a semi-protected alleyway to run up and down. Once closed up and with our truck drivers finding whatever cover they could inside their cabs, we tried to take back some control over the situation.

Now, you'll recall the girly screaming I mentioned earlier. Once the front was set and my counterpart from the second front GT took charge of that area to our front, I ran back through the secure alleyway to check on the rest of the team and our cargo truck drivers. The two, gun trucks in the middle, were in place perfectly and protecting both centre flanks, good. I kept running. I got to the arse end of the convoy to find Charlie (still hooked up to the Bobtail) and his other GT in place but still scrambling to get themselves sorted. Taking a second, I found out why.

The security guard we'd put in the Bobtail cab of the truck to focus the driver, had taken a round cleanly through the back of his skull directly through his helmet (I told you they were rubbish didn't I) and blown a fair chunk of his face off when it came out. In his blinding panic at seeing the guard's face pop open, the Bobtail driver had swerved all over the road whipping Charlie's gun truck left and right creating Charlie's high-pitched screaming over the radio in his attempts to get the security guard to control the driver. He wasn't listening, slacker!

When I arrived and surveyed the scene, taking in what had happened, Charlie was busy doing CPR on the poor sod, but he was three ways from fucked. Nice of them to try, but he was already dead, and we knew it. I did what I could by leaving them to do that and set their top mounted gunners with orders to look out and cover the rear of the convoy. I didn't hang about, the guard was dead, and Charlie was once again taking control of the rear, so I ran forward.

Let's not forget it was bloody hot. Summer in Iraq and 55°C on an average day. Add heavy body armour, mountains of ammunition, a Kevlar helmet and a few dozen pricks trying to kill you and you sweat pretty good. But I ran. I checked on the middle two GTs; I updated the expats about our KIA and then continued on my way. When I arrived, I was happy seeing my gun truck was still in place, and my gunners were still focused albeit with cigarettes now in hand. My GT had no choice in staying put: all four tyres were shot away. Its engine though was still running though by some small miracle, but it wasn't moving anytime soon.

We had laid down a heavy enough rate of return fire that by the time I got back to the front, the shooting had died down to a sporadic rate of pot shots from some wankers hiding in the scrub who thought they were snipers with some 20-year-old piece of shit AK that hadn't been cleaned in five years. Idiots.

About now a larger response from our US Military friends had started happening. Two lovely (and I mean they were fucking beautiful) Apache helicopter gunships arrived on the scene from the nearby Balad Air

Force base. The Yanks have many problems in their military, equipment is not one of them. The sound of those choppers arriving was the best sound ever.

Like Audie Murphy, any dipshit (with just three brain cells) who decides to take a pot-shot at Apaches, the result of which would for the next four seconds result in said dipshit being forcefully torn limb from limb by the forward mounted 20mm helicopter cannon as it responded in kind... OK, time to try to let the body slow down. My adrenaline is pumping, I started hoping I might make it out of this particular shit fight to see what happens next.

For those of you who don't know me I was a 'Tanky.' I proudly served in the New Zealand Army for eleven years. People can say whatever they like, but as those choppers circled watching over us, I was the proudest little tin can ever as four, yes four, M1A2 American Main Battle Tanks, weighing in at 68 tonnes each arrived at our location at speed. They literally shook the ground where we stood and took over the four corners of our beat-up little team, thus giving us the chance to regroup.

We checked on our team and our cargo drivers; we changed tyres, took stock of our ammo, smoked many cigarettes, drank a shit-ton of water and tried to smile. This had been a rough one and we all knew that 1 KIA was bad, but it was far, far better than what it could have been. Once we were ready, we were escorted (slowly) back to Balad. We were towing anything ruined beyond local help. We were literally driving on flat tyres as we didn't have enough spares. It was slow going. But I would guess we were the best protected convoy for that 30 km or so with two tanks front and rear and the two gunships still rotating above us.

Once secure inside Balad AFB, I took our guard to the hospital to be declared dead. The doctors and medics there were great, speedy, efficient and empathetic all at the same time. Thank you. Another of our GTs was sent away with a load of cash to return with pizzas, trays of fizzy pop and a full restock of smokes for the team. We ate and talked; it is weird how teams bond, at times like this.

Later that day, another team arrived laden down with spare tyres and more ammo for us. We fixed our shit, strapped our dead onto a pallet packed in ice, re-bombed our gun trucks and headed off back onto the same highway to make our way south once more. Because that's what convoys did, we dusted ourselves off, reloaded and got back to it.

This was just one of the multitudes of convoy Iraq tales I have. I spent fifteen years in Iraq and met some of the best people I will ever know. I'm here. I have all my fingers and toes and I have enough in my life to be happy.

PSD is for pussies! If you want to discover who you really are, do a convoy in some shithole, get brassed up and walk away knowing you've lived (even if it was for just a few minutes).

Tim's personal security tip: *Stay alert; you must always be ready for the unexpected. Stay focused and be on the lookout for any possible threats, no matter if you're in a shithole somewhere or walking the street with the dog while at home, always be ready.*

Melted Malted Bars

A quick and simple snack to enjoy as a treat at any time of the day when morale and energy levels are low. One thing Iraqis never go short on is chocolate, so ingredients are always available no matter where you find yourself.

INGREDIENTS:

1x box malt chocolate balls (or 4–5 small packets)

4x large chocolate fruit and nut bars

1x pkt oat biscuits to suit choice, (Hob Nobs Commando Biscuits for best results)

1x baking tray

1x saucepan

1x glass/porcelain mixing bowl large enough to sit on the saucepan

3–400 ml of water

METHOD:

Preheat a saucepan containing 3–400 ml of water until the water just starts to boil. Turn heat down to a simmer and place the mixing bowl on the saucepan.

Now break the bars of fruit and nut into small chunks and add to the bowl and allow to melt, stirring gently occasionally with a spatula. Once fully melted, add in the Maltesers and allow to melt, leaving a few out for final decorations. Turn the heat down.

Meanwhile, on the baking tray, using a rolling pin, smash up the biscuits into fine crumbs. Cover the whole tray evenly with this biscuit base. Now taking the melted chocolate, gently pour the contents over the biscuit base covering the tray evenly to the edges.

Add the Maltesers you set aside over the top for decoration and place into the fridge for an hour to cool. After cooling, remove and enjoy with friends.

The Private Volunteers

ALAN

- *Formerly*: Sergeant Royal Marines — Personal Protection Officer — Maritime Security Operator.
- *Saw active service in*: The Falkland Island war, Northern Ireland, Granada.
- *Seven years private security in*: Iraq, USA, Kurdistan and Cyprus.

As the sun set over the Tigris River in southern Iraq, the little gathering had been small in number but no less unique. They were a grizzled-looking group of men that sat there in that warm late afternoon talking over the tops of their beers. To look at them you'd be forgiven for thinking they were anything but average looking, their longer-than-usual hair of various colours, was matted and stuck out at jaunty angles, some of which had started to go grey at the temples. All of them had some kind of facial hair that ranged from days of stubble to moustaches and beards, of every type and description, growing every which way possible. All of them had their faces deeply lined with the pressures and trappings of operating in such a dangerous country, yet they were smiling and laughing, lost in each other's company. It was a rare sight to ever have any more than couple of us together at any one given time, yet here we were, six of us… and it was a magical moment.

We were sitting in a loose circle situated between two of the dirty-white mobile units that served as our accommodation. However, that didn't do anything to diminish a spectacular view of the Tigris River that flowed southbound lined with palm trees and the occasional fishing boat floating downstream. The afternoon was still warm, even as the sun started setting over the horizon, giving way to a magnificent range of colours that filled the sky like a painter's palette and adding further to the moment. In the middle of the group sat a single case of beer, which we all sat around like some magnetic holy altar that saw an occasional hand move in and take one, offering it around before the sound of the ring pull lifted... hssst!

At that time, working convoys in Iraq was arguably the most dangerous job on the planet. It was tough going; the pressures were insurmountable to the dangers of travelling the length and breadth of a complex and high-risk Iraq, often at incredibly slow speeds and through hostile territory. All of us in the group were old hands at job at this point and knew the dangers only too well, having worked for a number of years negotiating through mission after mission up and down the country. We had all lost people we knew along the way, but here and now was not the time for being morose and the conversation was light and full of laughter, as if no one wanted to be the one to spoil the moment. We all knew the dangers; we all knew that tomorrow might be our last and we accepted the way things were.

As we revelled in the moment, sipping beer, laughing and talking loosely on anything other than work, the case of beer began to run low, so I slipped away to my hooch and returned with yet another case I had kept hidden under my bed for just such a reason and I also returned with my guitar. Suddenly the mood of the group shifted to one of excitement and as the new beers were being passed around, I broke into the first few chords of a song I knew. Nobody else knew it, so after a chorus of "play us another one Shakey" I cracked into 'Dirty Old Town' by The Pogues. As we all sang merrily away, drank beer and watched the final colours dip into night time I smiled a big, daft grin on my face, possibly the first in a long time.

The next morning, I was up and heading to the laydown yard where I sought out my CET: Convoy Escort Team, of Iraqi gangsters as well as the cargo trucks we would be escorting up the line. My Iraqis had been with me for a while now and we were moulding into a tight-knit little unit. They knew how I liked to operate and with Robbie as my 2i/c, we were functioning as a single fluid unit. Many of my Iraqis had been former army and at least two had been on the front line during the Gulf War fighting against the allies, yet here we all were together on the same side, ironic!

After receiving my briefing from the Ops Room and getting any overnight intelligence, I made my way to the yard to find Robbie walking the line and checking cargo and trucks, contents and strappings. He reported that the trucks and drivers were ready to go and that they had enough fuel to reach the first way station. This was an important issue as some of the truck drivers were sneaky and it wasn't uncommon to see welded hidden fuel tanks underneath. All fuelling was courtesy of the US Army and drivers were known to fill both main and hidden tanks, to then sell the spare fuel on the black-market post-mission.

With the checks and all safety briefings done with the team, we mounted up and hit the road in one long snake of vehicles. Today we were transporting military vehicles to the Iraqi Army in Baghdad which was a simple two-day mission: up the line — drop off the cargo — overnight in Baghdad — and return. Elsewhere, some of our other colleagues were not so lucky and could be on the road for up to several days, dependent on their destination and cargo so we considered this mission a semi-decent one.

The going was laborious; often we travelled at excruciatingly slow speeds and staying together is an art form. There is endless chatter on the radio with command and control of the convoy, as well as the lead vehicle calling out any hazards and dangers he may spot. Then there is the tail-end Charlie (Robbie) calling out when the convoy had cleared the danger, plus calls from operations giving regular and updated information on recent activity. It was noisy to say the least.

Periodically a cargo truck would break down causing the convoy to slow to a stop that could see us stretched out over a kilometre in length. We would then go through a time-tested routine of giving the broken truck just twenty minutes to fix any issue. If successfully fixed then we would press on, but if not, then the spare Bobtail at the back of the convoy would come up and hitch to the trailer before we would press on, leaving the Iraqi driver with his broken truck. It was a necessary way of doing things as we were dangerously exposed and needed to think about the bigger picture of the many. Also, every Iraqi driver had the details of his company's recovery, brothers and cousins in the motor trade and areas dotted throughout Iraq where they could find lodgings for the night, so it wasn't all bad.

Meanwhile we cracked on, our top gunners constantly scanning left and right for hidden dangers such as ambushes or detonation wires that led to deadly IEDs planted at the sides of roads. It was always a gamble running convoys; we were vulnerable and in very flat, open country. We were miles from any support and so we kept at high alert constantly scanning as we progressed north.

It was around five p.m. when we reached Baghdad and already the sun was thinking about dipping in the sky. It was hot as hell in our armoured vehicles and everyone was dripping in pools of their own sweat. Regardless, we had made good progress as we travelled up through the Mansour district of Iraq's capital city. Halfway up the dual carriageway there was a cross-over bridge that historically, saw an Iraqi Police checkpoint situated on top control the traffic. The call came down the line that we were turning off, to then cross over to come back down the other side of the dual carriageway, as the Iraqi Army Camp was on the opposite side of the road just a kilometre south of where we had just come up from.

The police CP were a regular crew and often stopped traffic for international convoys like ours in an unwritten courtesy. In return, and as a means of thank you, we dropped off a case or two of water as it was crazy hot and those lads didn't have much. We called it 'paying our taxes' and a case of water was nothing to us if it meant we greased the wheels for others who followed suit.

I called down to Robbie, "Time to pay our taxes mate, can you do the honours?"

"Roger that" came the reply and he instructed his top gunners to ready themselves to hand over the boxes of water.

What happened next is etched in my mind forever and still makes me laugh to this day. As we came up the ramp to the junction, the police held up all the traffic and by the time Robbie's truck had arrived at the checkpoint, I was on the down-ramp on the opposite side looking back to make sure there were no issues. I watched as a small Iraqi policeman ran over to the rear gun truck and stretch his arms upwards to receive the box of water that the top gunners were gently lifting over the side of the rear armour plating. But the carboard must have been damp because what I saw next was the box suddenly giving way and *dink, dink, dink!* one by one the bottles fell through the bottom of the box and hit the policeman on his head with his arms still held aloft. As if that weren't bad enough, thinking his job done, Robbie's gun truck then accelerated forward and over the top of the fallen bottles cascading the policeman head to foot in a tidal wave of water. As we exited the ramp and back onto the dual carriageway, my last vision was one of a soaking wet policeman, looking skywards with a 'why me' expression on his face.

We reached the Iraqi camp and managed to track down the commander before we handed over the cargo with no issues. With all the necessary paperwork completed and signatures done, we left them to their new toys and cut through the city to our overnight camp. Sleep was impossible, as that night a salvo of mortars had targeted the American troops situated in the Green Zone just a couple of kilometres down the road from our camp. Alarms, tannoys and helicopters buzzed away into the early hours, before calm was once again restored.

The next morning after breakfast, we were up and ready to go. With everything sorted, radio checks made and with a call to our own southern Operations Room to inform them we were "moving," we headed out of the camp, slipped onto Route Irish and headed towards MSR Tampa that would take us south and away from Baghdad.

We had just cleared the Irish/Tampa junction when a call came up that one of the convoy trucks had broken down. So we pulled over to the side of the motorway and gave the driver his obligatory twenty minutes to sort his issue. This was a very dangerous place to stop as technically we were still inside Baghdad city limits and this was known to be an attack hotspot. We had just informed our Operations Room of the situation when there came an almighty *Boom!* behind us. I turned to see a plume of smoke arch high into the sky, showering the area with rubble, debris and lord knows what else. *Some poor bugger just caught a packet,* I thought as I reached for my phone once more to let Ops know. Later, we found out that an Iraqi Army Patrol of Humvees returning from Anbar province, less than a kilometre from our position, had triggered a roadside IED. The resulting blast had destroyed one of the vehicles killing its occupants and wounding many more, including those civilians in close proximity. What a senseless waste of life, I thought.

With the vehicle fixed, we pressed on ever southwards, travelling past treelines that slowly gave way to rolling open land. About an hour into the journey, we were making excellent time and made more so by the unladen freewheeling convoy. Up ahead came the call that we were heading into yet another Iraqi checkpoint and the convoy slowed and prepared to negotiate through. As the lead vehicle stopped parallel to checkpoint official, I watched as the official and the front team went through a tired routine of questions and answers, of explaining who we were and what we were doing, before handing over the volumes of official paperwork we travel with for these types of events.

Bugger! We were being pulled over for further inspection by the CP. The convoy slipped over to the right and I got out with all my paperwork and walked over to the checkpoint official and my own team Interpreter, Mohammed, a tall, thin gangly youth who had once worked for the US Army as a 'Terp' during the war.

The official looked bored as I handed over my Arabic-written, government-sealed document that gave us official permission to travel. But still he was unrelenting. He stared solemnly at my document excruciatingly slowly, as if contemplating every word on the page. Minutes ticked by and still he stood reviewing the page until Mohammed looked at the official, then down at the document and, taking the document in his hands, turned it around, the right way up. The official couldn't read and was merely pretending to read until Mohammed had spotted the ruse. Embarrassed and red-faced, the official quickly hurried us through the CP before one of us let slip the façade to his comrades. I giggled as I walked back to my truck… "Only in Iraq."

As the journey wore on, we slipped into mind-numbing boredom. The mind can only stay alert so long and try as you may to stay focused, eventually you start to slip into tiredness and what we called 'zoning-out'. Whole kilometres could pass by in a flash and you'd find yourself frantically trying to recall what you'd seen. There was a cackle of static as the radio flashed into life "... I spy with my little eye, something beginning with S..." I was glad I wasn't the only one who was bored!

At Italian Bridge, so-called because the Italian Military had rebuilt it after the war, we cleared the first checkpoint on the northern side and slowed to run over the ruts and potholes left neglected prior to going over the bridge. Traffic was heavy and packed on the bridge as we drove over the speed bump that led us onto the bridge itself. A civilian lorry and trailer were coming up on the opposite lane and was pushed hard over to the side as a faster car slipped up the inside to overtake. The lorry drove over what looked to be a small pile of rubbish gathered by the side of the road. There was a flash of light and an explosion as the roadside bomb detonated under the wheels of the lorry and put the northbound traffic into a frenzy. The trailer and inside car had caught most of the explosion, which effectively had shielded us as we continued onto the bridge. I checked that everyone was OK and we cracked on leaving the scene to the Iraqi Police and Army.

By mid-afternoon we were back in our camp and de-kitting and prepping the vehicles for the next mission, which was the next morning. We cut our team loose and reported to Ops that we were back in one piece. I wrote up the Incident Reports and went to find Robbie. He was sat in the same spot as before, watching the sun set over the Tigris River. He looked up at me, handed me a cold beer and said, "Go get your guitar, mate…"

Baghdad Munch Brunch

An outstanding meal for the team before or after a mission which will see them full and packed with energy. Group food was often a way of life for teams, sharing both the work load and the eating of meals all of which gave a real sense of togetherness, especially when a beer was conjured up with it.

INGREDIENTS:
Chicken or beef sausages enough for 4 persons
(Muslim countries are not likely to sell pork products)
1x tbls olive oil
1x clove garlic
Half tsp paprika
Pinch chilli powder
1x red pepper (chopped)
1x tin chopped tomatoes
1x tbls tomato puree
450ml chicken stock
175g pasta (your choice)
2x tbls double cream
2x tbls parmesan cheese (grated)

METHOD:

Chop the sausages into small 2cm chunks, then heat the oil in a frying pan before adding the sausages. Fry them until the sausages brown all over. You can break the sausages down smaller at this point should you want to.

Add in the garlic, fennel, paprika and chilli flakes and cook for another two minutes. Now add the tin of tomatoes, the tomato puree and chicken stock and bring all the ingredients to a simmer.

Add in the pasta and cook for another fifteen minutes until the pasta softens with occasional gentle stirring of the contents. Prior to serving, add in the parmesan cheese and double cream and cook for another two minutes allowing for the ingredients to blend and then, remove from the heat and allow to rest for two minutes.

Ladle into bowls and serve with warm bread and a big mug of tea. Delicious.

The Real Expendables

Scotty Grieg, Team Leader, Task Commander

Between 2006-2007, convoy work in Iraq was without a doubt the most dangerous job in the world. The press, the political opposition in Britain and the United States were asking questions. Why, in a war that supposedly ended four years earlier, were hundreds of our young troops still being killed and hideously maimed?

The solution was simple enough, just pay someone else to do the really high-risk dangerous jobs that where difficult to protect and easy to hurt. When a private security operator is killed by a roadside bomb, there is no flag-draped coffin to be ceremonially carried from the tailgate of an aircraft, no waiting press, no awkward political questions; we were The Real Expendables.

In the early days immediately after the 2003 war in Iraq, there were a few undesirables that managed to slip through the Human Resources net, some real horror stories of nightclub doormen, minders and so-called hard men, but they were easily found out and found lacking. Most of them couldn't find their ass with both hands, never mind organise and escort a convoy of ten cargo trucks, four, gun trucks and all the kit and equipment needed here between. To then travel through the desert at night, to some remote and obscure FOB (Forward Operating Base), that had no name on the map just a six-figure grid reference and through hostile and risky areas, was not for the faint of heart.

We were armed to the teeth, loaded with belt-fed vehicle mounted machine guns, state-of-the-art M4 assault rifles and B6 four-wheel-drive armoured vehicles, but we could still only move at the speed of the slowest and heaviest of trucks. On the MSR (Main Supply Routes) we were always time and place predictable, yet off road, the trucks were sometimes so slow that you could have got out and walked faster, that was only when they didn't bottom-out or get stuck in the sand. In short, we were sitting ducks but I won't lie, the money was good and to us it was worth the risk.

In October 2006, I lead one such convoy from the Abu Ghraib Warehouse in western Baghdad, into Baghdad itself and popping out to the military training centre in Kirkush which was east of Baghdad towards the Iranian border. It meant skirting around close to Baquba which, back then was a very dangerous part of the world, as militant activity was rife in the area. It was to be a long and perilous journey and we made sure each and every one of us was ready for every eventuality. That readiness and preparation would prove to be a life-saver.

The trip to, and through Baghdad was without incident, save for an occasional change of a flat tyre, or refuelling the vehicles but other than that, we were incident free. After passing the Iraqi capital, we headed along a small single lane some 5km from Baquba where the road that was pitted and potholed from years of neglect and weather.

As the convoy approached a single-track road, there was suddenly a lightning-white flash and the ear-splitting crack of military grade high explosives. The first cargo truck was instantly decimated: the whole front end of the huge tractor unit just vanished and the twisted wreckage that remained was in flames. With the tractor unit gone, the trailer had buried itself about four feet deep into the road. The two trucks behind ploughed hard and heavy into the wreckage crushing and trapping both drivers in the folded metal and plastic of the cab. Miraculously and most amazingly, the driver of the lead truck now in pieces, had been thrown clear of his vehicle by the blast, but the second driver was badly pinned inside his cab with both his femurs broken. His chest was crushed against the steering wheel and he was in a really bad way. The driver of the third truck was also trapped but had not suffered the same life-threatening injuries as the second driver.

If there was any chance of saving the trapped drivers, the team would have to move fast. The wrecked cab that was crushing him had to be pulled forward off his legs to make enough room to pull him free. The team brought one of the spare tractor units up from the rear of the static convoy and by connecting cargo chains to the front of the smashed cab began pulling the wreckage forward and off the driver's trapped and broken legs. I could see the pain the driver was in; it must have been excruciating but there was no alternative if he was to have any chance of surviving.

Just then my attention was drawn to the sound of gunfire coming from the rear of the convoy from an unknown number of AK-47s firing. This was immediately followed by our rear two belt-fed 7.62mm PKM machine guns opening up in response.

Steve's voice then crackled in my covert earpiece "Contact rear!"

From where I stood, I could hear the distinct sound of a gun-battle going on at the rear of the convoy, with both of our rear security vehicles firing bursts of their heavy calibre ammunition off into the distance.

This is taking too long, I thought. By now some of the other truck drivers had arrived and were in the melee along with the rest of the team trying to work the trapped driver's legs free without killing him. Nick punched an auto jet syringe of morphine into the top of the trapped man's thigh, but it seemed to have almost no effect; this guy really was in a bad way.

Our convoy was now taking sporadic small arms fire from the buildings left and right of us; the two front gunners, operating the lead PKMs, instantly traversed on their axis and battered down long bursts of accurate fire towards the flashes of rooftop gunfire, buying just a few more minutes we so desperately needed. Eventually, we freed the trapped driver; slowly and gently, we lifted him down from the cab. Nick slid the spinal board under the driver, quickly securing him with long Velcro straps around his body.

Steve was back in my earpiece: "Scotty we are getting bloody mullered back here bro; we are taking RPGs and belt-fed rounds and our gun trucks are taking a real battering; we need to move soon!"

Just then, two mortar rounds straddled the convoy landing in the soft ground at the side of the road sending plumes of dirt, smoke and debris sixty feet into the air.

"OK Steve we're moving now," Scotty ordered. "Bring your gun trucks up to me; if we can't go back, we need to keep pushing forward!"

Looking back along the road, I could see at least two of the middle cargo trucks were now in flames, but at least they had all the drivers with the security team and Steve was on his way along with his two, gun trucks and their mounted PKMs. Steve's battered gun trucks eased past the burning convoy and I could see what was left of the tyres flapping and slapping along the road, shredded to just flimsy pieces of rubber and only just still attached to the metal of the wheel rims. The bullet strikes in the thick armoured glass looked like huge silver Christmas snowflakes stuck to the windows.

We now quickly got organised. With everyone now on board our vehicles that could move, we were once again off and moving forward. We had just about managed another two hundred yards when the front gun truck triggered yet another roadside device, the explosion bringing our convoy to a grinding halt.

Along the road ahead, teams of militants were hastily wiring large artillery shells together in a daisy chain type IED, so as one detonated, it would trigger others, killing or maiming everything in its wake over a wide area. Militants then ran the command wire off to one side of the road and behind heavy cover, waiting for us to move. There was now no way forward and we were cut off from behind by the burning trucks with an increasing intensity of heavy small arms fire.

Scanning around, I noted to my right a set of heavy steel doors that led into the compound of a small school-type building. I aimed my gun truck right at the centre of the steel doors, then with just the right amount of throttle bumped the big doors open. The other three gun trucks followed close behind, and the forth rear gun truck then reversed against the doors holding them shut.

Here, inside the compound at least there was something to defend, the high whitewashed walls made the place look and feel like an isolated spot. If this was going to be our last stand then we, as the team were determined to give a good account of ourselves. That was probably an optimistic version of the situation—optimism usually being nothing more than the lack of credible alternatives.

The front doors to the school were locked. Two lads grabbed sledgehammers from the back of the gun trucks and began smashing their way in. But these were really heavy-duty doors and the sledgehammers weren't having much of an effect. With a change for a fresh set of arms on the hammers, two new lads set to it again. Just then a little old man appeared from out of nowhere and, with the door key in his hand and a nonchalant look as if nothing was happening around him, let us all in.

We secured the courtyard; Nick was still working hard on the casualties and doing a great job. Steve made his way onto the roof with three of the PKMs, closely followed by a few of the lads and as much ammunition as they could carry. I grabbed the remaining uninjured truck drivers and had them hand ball the rest of the team's ammunition from the gun trucks up onto the roof for Steve. All the while outside bursts of automatic fire would strike the sides of our defended building and Steve's three rooftop PKMs would instantly bark back a loud reply.

On the initial contact explosion, all four gun truck commanders, had initiated their tracker unit transponders, a vehicle alarm system that would set off bleeps, bells and whistles back in the main base operations office. The operations team back in Victor-2, in Baghdad, having now seen the alarms flash up on the main screens, were already busy putting rescue plans into action. From the roof of the building, Steve had a good signal for his satellite phone and was giving the Operations Room a complete situation report, and relaying the exact grid reference of their position from his GPS.

Victor-2 Operations then informed Steve that a US QRF (Quick Reaction Force) had been dispatched from

FOB Warhorse, about five miles away and four Humvees from the Seventh Calvary Division would be with them within thirty minutes. Our casualties were still breathing and the team were just about holding our own in this Alamo situation.

Gunfire raged on for agonising minute after minute around us. Eventually, four US army Humvees came trundling down the road towards us, the lead vehicle was punishing the insurgents mercilessly with his big 0.5mm Browning heavy machine gun, but inadvertently they were heading straight for the daisy chained IED by the side of the road, which we had spotted earlier. Our team had no direct radio communications with the military on the road below and no way of warning them of the danger they were heading into. I saw some of the team shouting and screaming at the Humvees to *"Stop-Stop-Stop"* but to no avail and still they came on.

And then... the inevitable happened: the lead Humvee triggered the first massive roadside bomb. The vehicle took the full force of the blast and everyone's heart sank in our little compound at the thought of the poor guys inside. After a moment or two, the US army QRF had no alternative but to self-recover back to FOB Warhorse.

As time wore on, the gun battle raged all around us. The PKMs on the roof were now beginning to run low on ammunition; I myself had gone through multiple magazines but was now dangerously down to my last three magazines, the others were not faring much better.

If something didn't happen soon, we would be unable to hold out for much longer.

Just then and not a moment too soon, a second US army QRF came storming down the road in four heavy armoured Bradley tracked personnel carriers, with two Apache helicopter gunships in close air support. The Bradleys hardly slowed as they made the tight turn into the small compound instantly rotating mechanically on their broad robotic tracks.

Once inside the compound, the Americans assisted us with the casualties, who were carefully loaded into the back of the Bradleys along with the remaining walking truck drivers. The rest of my team were then back in our battered gun trucks and we were off. The two Bradleys took the lead clearing a path by using their heavy calibre machine guns and led us back to FOB Warhorse, our four battered gun trucks in the middle and the remaining two Bradleys at the rear. The Apaches were still circling high overhead giving our convoy top cover.

Later in the day, a sister team from Abu Ghraib came up with a resupply of much-needed ammunition and tyres and we spent the night recounting our story with them. They sat agog as they listened intently to the details. We had been in a contact some three and a half hours and were virtually down to our last few magazines. We had escaped by the skin of our teeth with the loss of no one; even I blew out a long hard breath of relief at the thought of that, as we relayed the story to our colleagues.

The following morning the team was up at 0500 hours and back on the road two hours later with a new consignment of trucks and stores... If the wheels aren't turning you aren't earning!

Scotty's Personal Security tip. *"Shred and destroy all personal unwanted mail, letters, bills, etc. Knowledge is power so don't leave anything available that could be used against you. Especially your subscription to kinky gear dot com!"*